The Use of Hereford

A Medieval Diocesan Rite Reconsidered

William Smith

Acknowledgements: My thanks are due to my wife Helen for reading and commenting on this paper, and to Bishop Colin Buchanan, Dr James Steven and other members of the Alcuin Club Joint Liturgical Studies Editorial Committee for kindly accepting it for publication. Their interest is greatly appreciated.

2

Contents

1

Introduction

'I have endeavoured especially to show the different rites and the particular practices of the churches I have seen, and have every reason to believe that one will look upon them with some kind of satisfaction, and that those who travel in the places I mention will want to stop and hear High Mass or Vespers in the cathedral churches. They will then be edified by the ceremonies performed there, and, properly instructed, will have learnt the true meaning and spirit of the Church's rituals in its prayers.'[1]

The purpose of this monograph is to provide a *résumé* of the author's recent book,[2] which lists and discusses the known sources for the medieval Use of Hereford. While this lengthy work is intended to be as comprehensive as possible, there are inevitably areas that remain unexplored, in particular the musical aspects of the rite, here plainchant as found mainly in the thirteenth-century noted breviary[3] and the fourteenth-century gradual.[4] Since the author cannot claim to be a musicologist, this has to be left to those competent in this specialized field. His interest lies principally in the content and history of the manuscript and printed texts representative of the rite, especially the extant missals, breviaries and gradual that provide the mass and office portions integral to the Use of Hereford. The cults of saints associated with Hereford, in particular St Ethelbert and St Thomas Cantilupe, the Cathedral's principal *festa loci sancti* and focuses of pilgrimage even today,[5] have also been examined,[6] as well as vestments,[7] relics,[8] liturgical plate,[9] and processions.[10]

The nature and extent of the sources discussed at considerable length in the book will be examined here in less complex and more accessible detail. While sufficient has survived to allow some understanding of the distinctive features of the Use of Hereford, what remains is meagre in quantity and variety compared with the more copious material available for the medieval uses of Salisbury (more commonly known as Sarum) and to a lesser degree York. For Hereford one has to scratch around, so to speak, if one wishes to discover sources beyond those already familiar. While most of its surviving service-books, namely two of the missals (the printed edition of 1502 collated with one single manuscript),[11] breviaries, ordinal, collectar, and psalter[12] have long been known through dated and, by modern standards, unsatisfactory printed editions, the products of a less critical age of liturgical scholarship, the existence of other material is generally less familiar. Some of this will be examined here.

Before proceeding further, the term 'use' in a liturgical context should be explained. A 'use' may be defined as the local variation of a standard or parent rite, which in the West came to be regarded pre-eminently as the Roman Rite, particularly since the reign of Charlemagne (768-814). Early uses arose partly through the adoption of Gallican features by the Roman Rite as it became established throughout Europe, and partly through local developments in that Rite itself following its reform as a curial liturgy (that is, the liturgy of the papal court, or *curia*) during the pontificates of Innocent III (1198-1216) and his successor Honorius III (1216-27).[13] The great eras of cathedral building, the late twelfth and early thirteenth centuries, were decisive periods in the development of the distinctive local uses, which became consolidated and codified in customaries representative of the great churches in which they evolved. As collections of established liturgical customs these were as individual as the architecturally unique foundations that created them, with carefully worded directions relating to ritual and ceremony, vestments, and the regulation of feasts, including the local cults contributing to their spiritual and regional identity. Provided they did not conflict with the ancient traditions, customs and authority of the Roman Church in matters of doctrine, jurisdiction, discipline, and sacramental theology, uses were entirely acceptable, and indeed encouraged from early times, as valid local expressions of an historically evolved faith that formed the fabric of *ecclesia universa*. The chief characteristic of a liturgical 'use', therefore, was that it was representative of a particular foundation, usually a cathedral, and the area under its authority, usually a diocese.

---

1. 'Je me suis attaché principalement à marquer les differens Rits & les pratiques particulières des Églises que j'ai vûes; & j'ai tout lieu de croire qu'on les lira avec quelque sorte de satisfaction, & que ceux qui voyageant dans les mêmes lieux que je cite, voudront bien s'arrêter à entendre la grand' Messe ou les Vêpres dans les Églises Cathédrales, seront édifiez des ceremonies qui s'y font, parce qu'ils seront instruits & prévenus, & qu'ils auront appris les raisons littérales des pratiques & des cérémonies de l'Église, & son esprit dans ses prières' (Le Sieur de Moleon [Jean-Baptiste Le Brun des Marettes], *Voyages Liturgiques de France, ou Recherches faites en diverses Villes du Royaume ... contenant plusieurs particularitez touchant les Rits & les Usages des Églises: avec des Découvertes sur l'Antiquité Écclesiastique & Payenne* (Paris: Florentin Delaulne, 1718), Préface, iii).

2. William Smith, *The Use of Hereford, The Sources of a Medieval English Diocesan Rite*, 2015 (see Bibliography 1). Many of the references found in the book are omitted from this article.

3. Hereford Cathedral Library MS P. ix. 7, described by Frere, *The Hereford Breviary* 3, 1915 (see Bibliography 1) *passim* and especially lv-lxi; Mynors and Thomson, *Catalogue of the Manuscripts of Hereford Cathedral Library*, 1993 (see Bibliography 3), 124a-125b, with Plate 51; Smith, *Use of Hereford*, Ch. 4, *The sources*, I *Manuscript/Breviaries*, 241-2.

4. London, British Library Harley MS 3965 (Smith, *Use of Hereford*, Ch. 4, *The sources*, I *Manuscript/The Hereford Gradual*, 259-83).

5. Michael Tavinor, *Shrines of the Saints in England and Wales*, 2016 (see Bibliography 2), 152-8.

6. Smith, *Use of Hereford*, Ch. 14, *Principal Hereford cults*.

7. Ibid., Ch. 17, *Conclusion: 'Not entirely as they do at Salisbury'*, 694-6.

8. Ibid., Appendix II, *Primary and secondary relics, surviving and untraced, of St Thomas Cantilupe*.

9. Ibid., Appendix III, *Surviving and untraced medieval liturgical plate*.

10. Ibid., Appendix IV, *Hereford processions and processional crosses*.

11. Edited by Henderson, *Missale ad usum percelebris ecclesiae Herfordensis*, 1874 (see Bibliography 1).

12. The Hereford ordinal, collectar and psalter are discussed by Frere in addition to the breviaries (*The Hereford Breviary* 3, lxii-lxvii, with excerpts, 65-7, 68-81, 82-3, 84-9 (ordinal); lxvii-lxviii, with abstract of text, 3-36 (collectar); lxii (psalter), with collation in Hereford Breviary 1, 1-29); and Smith, *Use of Hereford*, Ch. 4, *The sources*, I *Manuscript/Ordinal/Collectar/Psalters*, 288-90 (ordinal), 291-305 (collectar), 306-12 (psalters), at 309.

13. Smith, *Use of Hereford*, Ch. 1, *Introduction*, 1.

2

British medieval dioceses
and their rites

During the Middle Ages, as today, dioceses belonged to ecclesiastical provinces under the jurisdiction of archbishops. Both before and after the Reformation England consisted of two provinces, Canterbury and York, with the four Welsh dioceses of St Davids, Llandaff, Bangor and St Asaphs created shortly after the Norman Conquest belonging to the former. Since its disestablishment in 1920 the Welsh Church, now comprising six dioceses, has been a separate province with its own archbishop. With the exception of Whithorn (Dumfries and Galloway) the ten Scottish dioceses created during the reign of King David I (1124-53) to supersede the now antiquated Gaelic Church (or Columban, after its association with St Columba of Iona, c.521-97) were subject to Roman authority, with St Andrews as the principal see. Founded around the year 900, St Andrews was subsequently re-established as a cathedral priory with a chapter of Augustinian Canons Regular in 1144, finally achieving full metropolitan status in 1472. Following the elevation of Glasgow as an archbishopric in 1492, Scotland henceforth consisted of two ecclesiastical provinces roughly dividing the country diagonally in two. With nine suffragans between them, Glasgow now incorporated Whithorn and Argyll, together with Sodor (The Isles, centred on Peel, Isle of Man, and later Snizort, Isle of Skye) and the Orkneys (Kirkwall). As separate dioceses Sodor (Suðreyjar) and the Orkneys (Kirkjuvagr) were originally subject to the extensive Norwegian archdiocese, or province of Nidaros (Niðaróss, now Trondheim), which also included

Iceland (with its two suffragan sees of Hólar and Skálholt overseeing the north and south of the country), the Faroe Islands (Kirkjubøur, or Kirkebo in Straumo), and Greenland (Garðar, or Gardar).

The medieval diocese of Hereford, our chief focus of interest here, was one of the smaller and more remote of the English sees. Extending into Shropshire and parts of Worcestershire, this was adjoined on its western boundaries by three Welsh dioceses (Llandaff, St Davids and St Asaphs), and on its eastern and northern limits by the dioceses of Worcester and Lichfield. Hereford was, and remains still, part of the Province of Canterbury, which covers about two thirds of England. By far the largest medieval diocese was Lincoln extending from the River Humber at its northern extremity to the River Thames in the south, where it was contiguous with the dioceses of Salisbury and London. The medieval Southern Province consisted of no fewer than eighteen suffragan dioceses; the Northern Province of York by contrast had only four, York itself, Durham (with its palatinate civil jurisdiction in addition to its ecclesiastical authority), Carlisle (from 1133), and Whithorn (from 1192 to 1492). Unity in matters of faith, worship, morals, and discipline was enforced by Canon Law (the *Corpus iuris canonici*), the universally binding ecclesiastical legislative code of the Roman Church. First appearing as a digest, or formally arranged collection, between 1230 and 1234, its decretals were supplemented in England by the synodical constitutions of the Province of Canterbury from 1222 to 1416 promulgated by successive archbishops from Stephen Langton to Henry Chichele. Their amalgamation as a five-part digest was completed in 1430 by the great canonist William Lyndwood as the basis of his famous *Provinciale* first printed in 1483,[15] which has continued as an authoritative source of English ecclesiastical law. During his distinguished career Lyndwood had been a canon of Hereford (prebend of Hunderton) from the 1420s until 1442, when he was appointed bishop of St Davids, where he died in 1446. Lyndwood was also employed in the royal service as Lord Privy Seal from 1432 to 1443. A very busy man indeed in an age when bishops customarily filled senior Crown appointments as officers of state.

Our interest in canon law is confined here to liturgical ordinances. While there was a canonical requirement for parish churches to observe the use of the metropolitan or principal church in its primary services of mass, vespers and matins, which theoretically determined the rite of its province or diocese, in practice it was not as simple as that. Of the seventeen medieval English cathedrals, seven (Canterbury (Christ Church), Ely, Winchester, Worcester, Rochester, Durham, and Norwich) were monastic, with their chapters served by Benedictine monks rather than secular canons. Almost unique to England, this arrangement, which lasted until the Reformation, was a consequence of the monastic reforms of the later tenth century associated with saints Dunstan, Æthelwold and Oswald. Of these, four (Canterbury, Ely, Winchester, and Worcester) were important pre-Conquest foundations with their own long-established liturgical traditions, which were transformed under Norman influence during the late eleventh and early twelfth centuries. Rochester and Durham, also pre-Conquest in origin but as secular institutions, were re-established as monastic foundations after their rebuilding in 1082 and 1093 respectively. The see of Norwich was created in 1094, with the construction of its great monastic church commencing two years later. With the archbishop or bishop as titular abbot, these seven cathedrals had, however, only the status of priories, with an elected prior as head of the chapter, despite their standing. This created an obvious rivalry between Christ Church (Canterbury) as metropolitan and St Augustine's Abbey, its near neighbour, to cite a well known example. Even though the more prominent Christ Church had been monastic even before its rededication by St Dunstan in 978, it still ranked only as a priory, albeit a cathedral. Apart from instances at Monreale in Sicily and Downpatrick in Ireland, the monastic cathedral appears to have been peculiarly English. With its chapter of Augustinian Canons Regular (or Black Canons), Carlisle (founded in 1133) was unique in England, its type of constitution occurring elswhere in Britain only in Scotland with the cathedrals of St Andrews and Whithorn (Premonstratensian Canons Regular, or White Canons). Wales had no monastic cathedrals, although in early times its four principal foundations (St Davids, Llandaff, Bangor and St Asaphs) were originally monastic institutions of the ancient Celtic *clas* type, which were dissolved soon after the Conquest and replaced by Norman administrative models, the broad structure of which still remains.

The form of the monastic rite, both in mass and office, would have rendered it unsuitable for secular diocesan use without considerable modification. The nature and extent of the rites followed by the monastic dioceses is a complex and still partially explored area. Investigations for Worcester, Norwich and Ely, however, have indicated the adoption of Sarum use from around 1300 adapted to the customs of their respective dioceses mainly on the evidence of calendars, litanies, missals, breviaries, and psalters. The same process was apparently also at work at Canterbury, though there is less substantial evidence for this diocese. Unlike the secular York rite, which was mandatory throughout the Northern Province, the monastic rite of Canterbury was confined to its cathedral. The implementation of Sarum use by the monastic cathedrals was effected relatively quickly and efficiently compared with the secular foundations of Exeter, Lincoln and London, for example, where change was apparently 'a more complicated, somewhat untidy, process, with clear indications of what could be called "resistance to Sarum", as Professor Nigel Morgan has remarked.[16] Reluctance on the part of these foundations to accept Sarum use no doubt represented an initial reaction against the perceived threat to their ancient traditions. The adoption of Sarum use by the monastic dioceses would have been a ready means of providing a conveniently available secular rite for their parish churches, for which the Benedictine services were clearly inappropriate. At the same time this would have been seen as an opportune way of conforming to the diocesan liturgical requirements stipulated by Canon Law.

The implementation of Sarum use by the monastic cathedrals as it had started to become more widespread from the early thirteenth century was part of a wider trend. More familiarly, this had also influenced and even superseded the rites of many of the secular cathedrals corresponding with the gradual adoption of Sarum constitutional practices towards the end of the twelfth century. At Exeter this twofold development was carried through at a later date by Bishop John de Grandison (1327-69), whose elaborate collection of Sarum-based ordinances appeared in 1337,[17] consolidating and developing the previous innovations of Bishop Walter de Bronescombe (1258-80). By contrast, Hereford and York remained aloof from Sarum in capitular governance, though in the former's case not entirely in its liturgy. York succeeded in maintaining its independence liturgically no less than constitutionally, as a comparison of its statutes and service-books, its missals and breviaries, in particular, with those of Sarum shows. Significantly, these were the two cathedrals that managed to preserve their own individual rites up until the close of the Middle Ages. While Hereford appears to display no sign of Sarum influence on its early statutes, its service-books present a very different picture, as will be discussed. Despite its apparent independence, Hereford use, as evidenced principally by its surviving missals and breviaries, showed itself open to Sarum influence from the mid fourteenth century, if not earlier. Yet in contrast with the other secular dioceses within the Province of Canterbury, which during this period came under the same influence, Hereford alone (apart from Salisbury, that is) succeeded in retaining its own distinctive rite, which will be considered next.

---

14. Ibid., Ch. 2, *The British diocesan rites: a brief survey*.
15. *Constitutiones provinciales Ecclesiae Anglicanae* (Oxford: Theodoric Rood, in-2°). The latest and best edition is *Provinciale, seu Constitutiones Angliae, continens constitutiones provinciales quatuordecim archiepiscoporum Cantuariensium, a Stephano Langtono ad Henricum Chicheleium, cum summariis et annotationibus revisum*, 2 parts (Oxford: H. Hall, 1679). For Lyndwood, see C. R. Cheney, 'William Lyndwood's *Provinciale*', *Medieval Texts and Studies* (Oxford: Oxford University Press, 1973), 158–84, and R. H. Helmholz, 'Lyndwood, William (c.1375–1446), administrator,

ecclesiastical lawyer, and bishop of St Davids', *Oxford Dictionary of National Biography* [ODNB]. http://www. oxforddnb.com/view/article/17264.

16. N. J. Morgan, 'The Introduction of the Sarum Litany into the Dioceses of England in the Thirteenth Century', in M. Prestwich, R. Britnell and R. Frame (eds.), *Thirteenth-Century England* 8, Proceedings of the Durham Conference, 1999 (Woodbridge: Boydell & Brewer, 2001), 179-206, at 199.

17. Exeter Cathedral Library MS 3502 (Smith, *Use of Hereford*, Ch. 1, *Introduction*, 2 nn. 8-10).

3

The Use of Hereford and its possible origins

Hereford was one of six English dioceses that retained their former ancient locations after the Conquest besides the primatial sees of Canterbury and York, the others being London, Winchester, Worcester, Rochester, and (from 1050) Exeter. This long continuity provided a strong sense of historical identity even before the building of the medieval cathedral was begun by Bishop Reinhelm (1107-15),[19] named in its fourteenth-century obit book as 'founder of the church' (*fundatoris ecclesie*) of Hereford.[20] Reinhelm's church was erected on a site just to the north of the old Anglo-Saxon minster, which, in a much repaired but still dilapidated state, appears to have continued in use up until his episcopate. The new foundation replaced the remains of 'the famous minster' (*þæt mære mynster*), as it is described in the *Anglo-Saxon Chronicle*,[21] built by Bishop Æthelstan (1012/13 x 1016-10 February 1056) probably between 1020 and 1040. This had been largely, though apparently not wholly destroyed by fire during the Welsh depredations of 24 or 25 October 1055 led by the renegade Earl Ælfgar with the willing help of King Gruffudd ap Llywelyn. Æthelstan's successor, the warrior bishop Leofgar (consecrated in March 1056, despite his canonically questionable martial inclinations), was slain by Gruffudd on 16 June the same year at Glasbury-on-Wye in Powys during a battle with the Welsh. The diocese was henceforth administered by Ealdred, bishop of Worcester, until the appointment of Walter of Lorraine as bishop by Edward the Confessor in 1060. Though unlikely to have been substantial, Æthelstan's minster had superseded an earlier, probably wooden structure dating from around 825. This originally housed the relics of St Ethelbert (Æthelberht, Æþelbryhte, Æðelbryhte), the adolescent king, or sub-ruler (*regulus*), of the East Angles murdered at the instigation of King Offa of Mercia in 794, who henceforth became patron and titular of Hereford Cathedral, together with the Blessed Virgin. The deposit of royal relics at Hereford, a political no less than a devotional act, established its church as the saint's cult centre and a prominent place of pilgrimage both before and after the Conquest. The apparent loss of the relics in 1055,[22] however, seems to have led to a decline of the cult, though efforts were made to promote it during the late twelfth century by a *Life* of the saint written by Gerald of Wales and the quest for new relics. Pilgrim attendance at Hereford was significantly greater from the end of the thirteenth century following the development of the cult of St Thomas Cantilupe (1218-82), whose relics were also enshrined in the cathedral, which became the most important pilgrim centre in the West of England after the second translation of his relics there in 1349. His cult continued to flourish until its cessation at the Reformation, with significant developments after 1420 following the centenary of his canonization, which appears to have been celebrated by musical elaborations to the liturgy and the establishment of a weekly mass in his honour.

It may be speculated whether there was any liturgical continuity between the old Anglo-Saxon Hereford minster and its post-Conquest successor in the manner of the early monastic foundations of Canterbury, Ely, Winchester and Worcester. The scale of events of 1055, when Bishop Æthelstan's church was destroyed, suggests that this was unlikely. Investigations here are made difficult by the few surviving liturgical sources from this period. These are limited to the late eighth- or early ninth-century Hereford Gospels[23] and a mid eleventh-century gospel-lectionary, or *evangeliarium*,[24] a collection of gospel excerpts arranged in narrative order rather than according to the liturgical days of the year, perhaps for the purpose of preaching or teaching. The Gospels are famous as the oldest manuscript in the cathedral library and the only known pre-Conquest Hereford book to have survived the Welsh depredations *in situ*. The gospel-lectionary has associations with Bishop Æthelstan, whose Old English description of the eastern bounds of the diocese are recorded in it, but it may have originated at Worcester. A troper,[25] a book containing musical embellishments to select texts of the mass or office (such as the *Gloria* and *Kyrie eleyson*), dated around the same period as the gospel-lectionary, is now believed to be of Worcester or Canterbury rather than Hereford provenance and may therefore be discounted. In any event, though significant in its own right, the tenuous evidence provided by the first two of these three manuscripts is insufficient to form any coherent idea of the pre-Conquest Hereford liturgy.

In his survey of the surviving sources the author hoped to gain some insight, if only limited, into the pre-history of the Use of Hereford, that is, its form and content antedating those represented by its later service-books. Such an enquiry, indeed, might be pursued against the wider question of the origin of the English diocesan rites in general, all belonging to the same broad Western liturgical family. Pre-eminent in England was the Sarum rite, which over a century and a half ago was believed to have derived from Rouen, the primatial see of Normandy. The tradition associating its origin with Osmund of Sées (from 1457 St Osmund), first Norman bishop of Salisbury (1078-99), was long accepted and continued to be taken for granted by the Victorian liturgists, such as the Anglican William Palmer (1803-85) and the Catholic Daniel Rock (1799-1871), until 1886, when a voice of dissent was raised by the Catholic Edmund Bishop.[26] In his review of the second edition of Albert Pearson's *The Sarum Missal done into English* published in 1884[27] doubt was cast on the old and unfounded assumptions regarding Rouen derivation discussed in its introduction. Over a decade later the Anglican Walter Howard Frere[28] published the first part of his influential

Use of Sarum in 1898,[29] which raised further issues concerning Sarum origins. With its analysis and discussion of Sarum customs as presented in its selectively edited texts of the consuetudinary, customary and ordinal,[30] material was now available for a more informed and critical understanding of this principal medieval English rite. Among other unsubstantiated assumptions, its traditional attribution to Osmund was radically called into question, representing a misunderstanding that, according to Frere, 'seems simply to have grown out of the association of his name with the Consuetudinary; it ... [being] not probable that it can rest upon some independent evidence which is no longer extant'.[31] Indeed, 'the Consuetudinary, as it stands, is not the work of St Osmund',[32] though Frere acknowledges that it incorporates elements which may be fairly ascribed to him.[33]

Yet while the views of Palmer, Rock, Pearson and others on Sarum origins were beginning to be regarded as questionable even in their own age, they were understandable at a time when the critical study of medieval liturgy was still in its early stages. On the constitutional side the English secular cathedrals had certainly drawn on Norman models in the establishment of their personnel in the so-called 'four-square' capitular organization of dean, precentor, chancellor and treasurer, an arrangement that continues, with modifications according to place and circumstance, to this day. Liturgically, direct Norman influences might also be seen to have been at work, with Rouen, the primatial church of Normandy, as a likely source. If specific instances are sought, however, it is precisely here that these assumptions break down. As, indeed, it is now recognized that the constitutions of the English secular cathedrals appear to have developed as the result of eclectic borrowing from their Norman counterparts over a long period, so it now appears that their liturgies evolved along similar general lines. The process is thus one of slow and steady growth over time, adapting, modifying and reshaping according to circumstances, custom or necessity until the introduction of printed service-books during the late fifteenth and early sixteenth centuries crystallized and standardized to a considerable degree the various local rites. Thus, Bishop was correct in his criticism of Pearson's statement that 'the use of Rouen and that of Sarum were almost identical in the eleventh century,'[34] for the supposed similarities between these two rites are merely those common to the substructure of all medieval Western rites and cannot, therefore, be cited in support of an assumed ancestry. Nor are comparisons with other Norman rites any more helpful. Where Rouen fails, Bayeux, for example, might be seen as the next likely candidate, but even here, as Frere has shown, no satisfactory conclusions can be drawn. Indeed, the rites of Bayeux and Sarum, 'though similar, are also very different', the number of the variations being, moreover, 'of a somewhat fundamental sort'.[35]

An investigation of Hereford origins was first made by Edmund Bishop in 1893 in an important article reprinted posthumously in *Liturgica Historica*, the collection of his research papers published in 1918, the year after his death.[36] In 'Holy Week Rites of Sarum, Hereford, and Rouen Compared' Bishop develops his earlier critique of Pearson, noting that 'the source of the special features of the Sarum ceremonial must be sought for elsewhere than at Rouen'.[37] By subjecting the forms of the three Holy Week rites (particularly that of Palm Sunday) to close scrutiny, Bishop discovered considerable divergences between Sarum and Rouen, but a notable similarity between Hereford and Rouen. This suggested to Bishop that, so far as the Holy Week ceremonial at least was concerned, Hereford seems to have derived parts of its liturgy from the use of the primatial church of Normandy. While no attempt was made to compare and analyse the other rites of these churches, it was concluded in respect of the missals that, 'it is impossible to go far in the work of confronting the texts without observing that, where differences occur among the three, the balance of agreement is between Rouen and Hereford rather than between either and Sarum'.[38]

Bishop's statement, however, requires some qualification, for he was comparing sources representative of the three rites 'as they stand at the close of the fifteenth century',[39] especially in the case of Hereford and Sarum, the early printed missals.[40] This is significant, for one result of the author's study has been to show that the first and only printed Hereford missal of 1502 is the product of considerable assimilation to Sarum, particularly in its ordinary and canon, and the prayers of the mass propers (the collects, secrets and postcommunions). Had Bishop, like his contemporary John Wickham Legg at a later date, undertaken a fuller comparison of the sources reviewed,[41] he would have found that the printed Hereford missal falls, as it were, between two stools, having affinity with the contemporary Sarum and Rouen missals, though being probably closer to the former. This does not alter the validity of Bishop's argument concerning the Holy Week rites, which at Hereford indisputably show apparent Rouen influence in certain particulars, but it does put the relationship between the sources concerned in a somewhat different perspective. A comparison with London, British Library Additional MS 39675 (known as the 'Dewick Missal' after its former owner Edward Samuel Dewick[42]), the earliest known Hereford manuscript missal (dated 1320 x 1349)[43] then in private possession and apparently unknown to Bishop, and the one least influenced by Sarum, would certainly have yielded very different results.

The origin and nature of the early post-Conquest Hereford rite remain unclear, but seem most likely to have been associated with the late eleventh-century Norman restoration of the cathedral. Apart from Bishop Reinhelm's rebuilding of the church, the earliest known post-Conquest regeneration at Hereford, was undertaken by his predecessor but one, Robert the Lotharingian (1079-95),[44] a notable mathematician and astronomer with interests in computation and chronology. With his more practical concerns, including what today would be termed estate and personnel management, it is very likely that Robert was responsible for compiling the original Domesday returns for the church of Hereford submitted in 1086. A restorer of the episcopal estates and reformer of the cathedral community, Robert also established and endowed a bishop's double collegiate chapel adjoining the old minster after a type associated with royalty and archbishops since the time of Charlemagne. Architecturally contrasting with contemporary English styles, this elaborate, square-form, two-storey foundation was dedicated on the lower level to St Mary Magdalene and on the upper to St Katherine of Alexandria. The chapel is said by the twelfth-century monastic historian William of Malmesbury to have been modelled on the imperial basilica at Aachen in Robert's native Lotharingia, an area broadly comprising the present Netherlands, Belgium, Luxembourg, Lorraine, Alsace, and north-west Germany. Regrettably, this splendid little edifice was demolished between 1738 and 1746 on the orders of Bishop Henry Egerton, whose actions rightly earned him the condemnation of the Society of Antiquaries. Though in a dilapidated state, it was still standing in 1721, when the antiquary William Stukeley made notebook sketches of it,[45] recording at the same time the shrine of St Thomas Cantilupe in the north transept of the cathedral, and St Ethelbert's Well.[46] The choice of St Katherine as co-titular is unusual at this early period and supports the suggestion that Robert introduced her cult at Hereford, probably establishing that of St Mary Magdalene at the same time. This may account for the appearance of other Eastern Mediterranean saints in the Hereford calendar, such as Antony (*festum* 17 January), Ignatius (*festum* 1 February) and Margaret of Antioch (*festum* 20 July), whose cults were then becoming popular in Lotharingia. The closeness of Aachen to Robert's hometown of Liège (where he appears to have been a cathedral canon), which lies about twenty-five miles (approximately 40 kilometres) to the south-west as the crow flies, suggests that he would have been familiar with the style of the palatine chapel and probably also with its elaborate symbolic liturgy focused on the emperor as God's anointed. Although most of the imperial palace no longer exists, its domed, octagonal chapel has been incorporated into Aachen Cathedral, famous as the burial place of Charlemagne and as a monument to the splendour of the Carolingian Renaissance. A similar and more contemporary structure, probably known also to Robert, would have been the episcopal double chapel (*Doppelkapelle*) of St Emmeram and St Katherine built on the south side of Speyer Cathedral between c.1080 and 1090. Robert would likewise have been familiar with the two-storey double collegiate church of St John at Liège established by Notker, prince-bishop of Liège, 972-1008.

The liturgy of the palatine chapel at Aachen is important as the predecessor of the rite of the papal *curia* during the early thirteenth century. The liturgical movement that arose as a result of the Ottonian Renaissance saw Lotharingian service-books brought into Italy during the second half of the tenth century, where they had a formative influence on the developing Roman rite, most notably with regard to the pontifical and order of the mass. Lotharingian sources thus played a crucial part in the history of the Western liturgy, which owes much to its German ancestry, and which looked to the rite of the imperial basilica as its principal model. It is likely that, in due course, these sources influenced the local variants of the Roman Rite practised in other prominent ecclesiastical centres in northern no less than southern Europe, which may have had consequences for the the development of the early Hereford rite.

The construction of such an ambitious and evidently costly building for personal devotion at Hereford suggests that Robert, in keeping with his evident awareness of *Liègeois* ecclesiastical patronage and hierarchy, may have introduced at the same time service-books of the type then employed in the imperial basilica at Aachen, or even perhaps his own cathedral of St Lambert at Liège. These would have been intended for use by his four chaplains and perhaps even the adjacent cathedral chapter then in the stages of reorganization. It has been suggested, indeed, that Robert may have intended his chapel to become a larger collegiate foundation in due course, thereby in turn developing the liturgical potential of the cathedral. This juxtaposed establishment, however, was not allowed to continue in its independence beyond the mid thirteenth century, by which time it had been granted in its entirety by the bishops to the dean and chapter, who were henceforth responsible for appointing its chaplains. Prominent among Robert's putative service-books would have been the plenary missals (*missalia plenaria*) as they had eventually developed from the Frankish 'mixed' Gregorian/Gelasian sacramentaries by the eleventh century. Augmented descendants of the early Gregorian books famously associated with Alcuin (c.735-804), these may have been the ultimate source of the earliest Hereford missals, if not of Robert's time then perhaps of the next generation or two, the distant ancestors of the known manuscript and printed missals representative of the later medieval Hereford rite. Their possible introduction by Robert accords with his reforms of the cathedral, which included the provision of library and probably also liturgical books, the appointment of its first known dean and other dignitaries, and apparently also the establishment of a bishop's chancery with a scriptorium for writing charters. Early capitular re-organization at Hereford, however, seems to have preferred Norman rather than the more rigid Lotharingian exemplars based on the rule of Chrodegang of Metz (c.755) as promulgated by the Council of Aachen for the Frankish Church in 817. Robert's friendship with Osmund, bishop of Salisbury, with whom, together with most of his other episcopal colleagues, he sided against Archbishop Anselm at the Council of Rockingham in February 1095 during the Investiture controversy, may have influenced this preference. Robert would certainly have been aware of Osmund's Norman-based capitular reforms at Old Sarum, which were eventually adopted as administrative models by other cathedrals throughout the British Isles.

Liturgical and capitular innovations were also in progress at Wells and Exeter during this period of widespread ecclesiastical reform. Robert's Lotharingian contemporary Giso introduced the cults of a number of Continental saints at Wells on the evidence of a surviving calendar,[47] as well as a canonical rule for his chapter probably based on that of Chrodegang of Metz. At Exeter the main part of the Leofric Missal[48] famously acquired for the cathedral by Bishop Leofric, who was brought up and educated in Lotharingia, was of north-east French (Arras-Cambrai region) origin, while his own copy of the rule of Chrodegang (the *Regula canonicorum*) in Old English and Latin imposed on his chapter still survives.[49] Other manuscripts of Exeter provenance associated with Leofric and apparently showing strong Lotharingian influence include a collectar,[50] a psalter,[51] and a pontifical.[52]

The idea of Robert as a liturgical innovator, therefore, should not be discounted, since a reorganized cathedral with revised service-books and a reliable calendar with dates and feasts for the ecclesiastical year would have been characteristic of his reforms of both church and diocese. In keeping with his computistical and astronomical interests probably developed while at Liège, the new calendar is likely to have been compiled in accordance with European chronological theories then current. Like the astronomer Roger of Hereford decades after him renowned for his computus, or mathematical tables, using the new Arabic numerals for calculating the date of Easter, Robert was also interested in astrology and its application. Anticipating Roger, he would likewise have been familiar with the most recent scientific ideas contributing to the universal advancement of knowledge. Due to Robert's initial inspiration Hereford developed into a prominent centre of learning during the twelfth century, with an international reputation for the teaching of arithmetic, geometry, music, and astronomy comprising the quadrivium, as this part of the medieval curriculum was called, as well as the dubious art of divination known as geomancy. Hereford could thus claim to be at this period 'the instructress of the Western regions' in the manner of Iona, to quote from Dr Samuel Johnson's famous account of the Holy Island in his *Journey to the Western Islands of Scotland* first published in 1775. Aspects of Robert's reforms, both calendrical and administrative, would have established themselves in due course as local customs later associated with the distinctive Hereford 'use' that defined the cathedral's liturgical and constitutional identity. By choosing to build his new chapel in imitation of one of the most famous imperial ecclesiastical foundations in

Europe, Charlemagne's basilica, Robert was surely aware of the symbolic relationship between worship and architecture, with its obvious spiritual implications. This was exemplified both in the grand style at Aachen and more modestly at Hereford with the simpler Carolingian ambience of the new episcopal chapel supplemented by Lotharingian service-books and an up-to-date liturgical calendar.

The work of liturgical innovation at Hereford may also have been continued by Robert's brother and successor Gerard (1096-1100), who was suitably placed to introduce Rouen practices there. Well connected as the nephew of Bishop Walkelin of Winchester (1070-98) and his brother Abbot Simeon of Ely (1082-93), Gerard became cantor of Rouen Cathedral early in his career and perhaps also archdeacon by 1091. It is not unlikely, therefore, that he would have benefited Hereford with his liturgical knowledge and experience during his time as bishop, augmenting with Norman ceremonial and texts the Lotharingian-style rite perhaps already established there by his predecessor. Gerard's episcopate may therefore represent an era of liturgical development, of eclecticism and experimentation probably characteristic of the cathedral rite of this era, which continued to evolve with the foundation as it grew in size and importance, and which appears to have established itself as a distinctive 'use' by the mid thirteenth century. This period coincides with the episcopate of Peter of Aigueblanche (1240-68),[54] who was probably responsible for the liturgical revision apparently underlying the Hereford noted breviary,[55] which may be dated between 1262 and 1268. Described by the American liturgist Richard Pfaff as 'the fullest English secular breviary of any use that survives from the thirteenth century',[56] this is important as the earliest known complete witness to the cathedral rite previous to further developments believed to have taken place during the episcopates of John Trillek (1344-60/1) and John Trefnant (1389-1404).

Yet whether Lotharingian beginnings, Norman influences, or, as might be the case, a combination of both are proposed, these suggestions can really be no more than speculations in an attempt to seek the origins of the Hereford rite, whose beginnings must remain obscure in the absence of firm evidence. At Hereford, no less than elsewhere, the form and structure of the liturgy developed together with the post-Conquest cathedral, which provided the essential architectural setting for its performance, the symbolic backdrop for its enactment, the stage for the unfolding of the sacred drama. Individual diocesan rites were therefore as unique as the great foundations in which they originated and evolved, and for which they were gradually consolidated and codified, a consideration that makes the rich liturgical diversity of medieval Europe comprehensible.

---

18. Smith, *Use of Hereford*, Ch. 3, *The Use of Hereford*.

19. Julia Barrow, 'Reinhelm (d. 1115), bishop of Hereford', *ODNB*. http://www.oxforddnb.com/view/article/95040.

20. Oxford, Bodleian Library MS Rawlinson B. 328, fol. 43r (under 28 October [1115]).

21. *The Anglo-Saxon Chronicle, a collaborative edition, a semi-diplomatic edition with introduction and indices*, general editors David Dumville and Simon Keynes (Cambridge UK: D. S. Brewer, 1983 ff.): vols. 1 Facsimile of MS F, the Domitian Bilingual, ed. David Dumville; 3 (MS A), ed. Janet M. Bately; 4 (MS B), ed. Simon Taylor; 5 (MS C), ed. Katherine O'Brien O'Keeffe; 6 (MS D), ed. G. P. Cubbin; 7 (MS E), ed. Susan Irvine; 8 (MS F), ed. Peter S. Baker; 10 *The Abingdon Chronicle, A.D. 956-1066* (a reconstructed edition of MS C, with reference to MSS B, D, E), ed. Patrick W. Connor; 17 *The Annals of St Neots with Vita prima Sancti Neoti*, ed. David Dumville and Michael Lapidge [*ASC*, cited by MS and year]: C, D 1055.

22. John of Worcester records that the relics of St Ethelbert and other saints were destroyed in the burning of the minster that year (*The Chronicle of John of Worcester* 2 (*The Annals from 450 to 1066*), ed. R. R. Darlington and P. McGurk, with translation by Jennifer Bray, *Oxford Medieval Texts* (Oxford: Clarendon Press, 1995), 576-9 *sub anno* [1055], (xvi) 1077). The Anglo-Saxon Chronicle (C 1055), however, states that Earl Ælfgar's marauders 'stripped and robbed' (*beryptan 7 bereafodan*) the minster of its 'holy things' (*haligdome*) and other treasures with no specific reference to destruction by fire, though the town itself (*ðam porte*) is said to have been burnt down. *ASC* D 1055 relates that they 'seized all the treasures in there [the minster] and led them away with them' (*namon þærinne ealle þa maðmas 7 mid heom aweglæddon*) after burning down the church and killing all the priests inside and many others (see also *infra* note 60). Two relics, however, the head at Westminster Abbey and a tooth at Hereford Cathedral, had apparently survived into the later Middle Ages (Smith, *Use of Hereford*, Ch. 14, *Principal Hereford cults*, at 612, 614).

23. Hereford Cathedral Library MS P. i. 2.

24. Cambridge, Pembroke College Library MS 302.

25. London, British Library MS Cotton Caligula A. xiv, fols. 1-36, the 'Caligula Troper', also known as the 'Cotton Troper'.

26. N. Abercrombie, *The Life and Work of Edmund Bishop*, 1959 (see Bibliography 1); R. J. Schoeck, 'Bishop, Edmund (1846–1917), liturgical scholar and ecclesiastical historian', *ODNB*. http://www. oxforddnb.com/view/article/31903.

27. *Dublin Review*, 3rd Series (July 1886), 199-203 (Smith, *Use of Hereford*, Ch. 1, *Introduction*, 8, with n. 44). The first edition of Pearson's work appeared in 1868.

28. H. B. Green, 'Frere, Walter Howard (1863–1938), bishop of Truro and liturgical scholar', *ODNB*. http://www.oxforddnb.com/view/article/33274.

29. See Bibliography 1.

30. The consuetudinary is edited from two manuscripts of the first half of the thirteenth century and two of the early fourteenth (Frere, *Use of Sarum* 1 (1898), xliv-liii). The six manuscripts of the customary and ordinal are of the fourteenth and fifteenth centuries (ibid., lvi-lviii). Frere compares the texts of the consuetudinary and customary by arranging them in parallel columns (ibid., 1 ff.).

31. Frere, *Use of Sarum* 1, xvii.

32. Frere, *Use of Sarum* 1, xvii. In its original form the consuetudinary is believed to date from c.1210 and to be 'the closing work of Richard Poore as Dean rather than his early work as Bishop' (ibid., xx).

33. Ibid., xviii, with reference to H. Bradshaw and C. Wordsworth (eds.), *Lincoln Cathedral Statutes* 3 [= pt. 2. ii] (Cambridge: Cambridge University Press, 1897), 860-88.

34. Albert Pearson, *The Sarum Missal done into English*, 2nd edn. (London: The Church Printing Co., 1884), xxiii.

35. W. H. Frere, 'The Connexion between English and Norman Rites', *Journal of Theological Studies* 4 (14), Old Series (1903), 206-14 (reprinted in J. H. Arnold and E. G. P. Wyatt (eds.), *Walter Howard Frere, A Collection of his Papers on Liturgical and Historical Subjects*, Alcuin Club Collections 35 (London, 1940), 32-40, at 40), at 214.

36. See Bibliography 1.

37. Edmund Bishop, *Liturgica Historica, Papers on the Liturgy and Religious Life of the Western Church*, ed. R. H. Connolly and K. Sisam (Oxford: Clarendon Press, 1918), 276-300, at 278.

38. Bishop, 'Holy Week Rites of Sarum, Hereford, and Rouen Compared', at 300.

39. Ibid.

40. For Rouen Bishop followed a seventeenth-century printed edition of a manuscript ordinal (*ordinarium*) of around 1450 and the processional of 1645, said to be 'the last to represent the traditional [Rouen] rite' ('Holy Week Rites of Sarum, Hereford, and Rouen Compared', at 278).

41. Legg's comparison of the early printed Hereford, Sarum and Rouen missals is in the third part of his *Missale ad usum Ecclesie Westmonasteriensis*, London, Henry Bradshaw Society 1 (1891), 5 (1893), 12 (1897). The printed Rouen missal used is that of 1499 (*Missale secundum usum insignis ecclesie Rothomagensis* (Rouen: Jean Richard and Martin Morin, in-folio).

42. Dewick bequeathed this missal to the British Museum (now British Library) in 1915, together with three other liturgical manuscripts (Smith, *Use of Hereford*, Ch. 4, *The sources*, I *Manuscript/ Missals*, 133, with n. 548). This is classified as a British Library Select Manuscript requiring special permission to examine it.

43. Apart from one twelfth-century (second half) fragment, that is (see *infra* note 66).

44. Julia Barrow, 'Robert the Lotharingian [Robert de Losinga] (d. 1095), bishop of Hereford', *ODNB*. http://www.oxforddnb.com/view/article/17026.

45. Oxford, Bodleian Library MS Top. gen. d. 13, fols. 47-50.

46. Ibid., fol. 46.

47. London, British Library MS Cotton Vitellius A. xviii, fols. 3-8v.

48. Oxford, Bodleian Library MS Bodley 579.

50. London, British Library Harley MS 2961 (the Leofric Collectar).

51. London, British Library Harley MS 863.

52. London, British Library Additional MS 28188.

53. *A Journey to the Western Islands of Scotland*, with James Boswell, *The Journal of a Tour to the Hebrides* (London: The Folio Society, 1990), 117.

54. N. Vincent, 'Aigueblanche, Peter d' [Peter de Aqua Blanca] (d. 1268), bishop of Hereford and royal councillor', *ODNB*. http://www.oxforddnb.com/ view/article/22015.

55. Hereford Cathedral Library MS P. ix. 7.

56. Richard W. Pfaff, *The Liturgy in Medieval England: A History* (Cambridge: Cambridge University Press, 2009), 470.

4

Surviving sources representative
of the Use of Hereford

Having considered the possible origins of the Hereford rite as it may have begun to develop from the late eleventh century, its surviving sources will now be briefly considered.

1 Manuscript[57]

Lack of evidence makes it uncertain whether there was any continuity at Hereford between the old Anglo-Saxon liturgy and its post-Conquest successor possibly established by Bishop Robert of Lotharingia, though early elements may have persisted. No sources are extant from the pre-Conquest period, apart from the late eighth- or early ninth-century Hereford Gospels[58] and the eleventh-century gospel lectionary[59] of disputed provenance but with apparent Hereford associations, as noted. The Gospels are believed to have belonged to the old Hereford minster during their later pre-Conquest history, and possibly also the lectionary. These two sources may therefore represent a precious, if tenuous, liturgical link with Æthelstan's early foundation, despite its being burnt down and 'stripped and robbed of holy things, of robes and of everything', in the sombre words of the *Anglo-Saxon Chronicle*.[60] A late eleventh-century part *Biblia Latina* may be a survival from Robert of Lotharingia's time,[61] though its provenance is uncertain.

The following century yields another gospel-book (*evangeliarium*), though of uncertain provenance;[62] a *Passionale sanctorum*, with readings for saints' days;[63] a homiliary (*homiliarium*) for the proper and common of the saints;[64] two stray antiphoner leaves, possibly of Hereford origin;[65] and a fragment of a parish missal from Much Marcle in Herefordshire.[66] No further sources are available until the second half of the thirteenth century, when the noted breviary,[67] the earlier part of the ordinal,[68] and a fragment of another breviary perhaps associated with the cathedral[69] make their appearance. A *Biblia Latina*,[70] dating from the beginning of the thirteenth century, is of unknown provenance but may have been later presented to the cathedral by Bishop Lewis Charlton (1361-9). For the earliest known missal of any substance one has to wait until the second quarter of the fourteenth century, between 1320 and 1349.[71] Later sources consist of three more missals, two for altar use dating from the first half of the fifteenth century;[72] three breviaries of parish or personal use dating from the fourteenth and fifteenth centuries;[73] the later part of the ordinal;[74] a gradual;[75] a collectar;[76] two psalters;[77] an obituary with martyrology;[78] a calendar;[79] a customary of capitular and prebendal interest;[80] and numerous liturgical fragments discovered in the cathedral library and the Herefordshire county and diocesan record offices, the references to which will be found in the author's book. Among these fragments are leaves of missals, breviaries, ordinals, graduals, and pontificals used as wrappers for archives, such as ecclesiastical court books and manorial records, or as pastedowns and fly or end leaves to manuscripts and early printed books. Some of these fragments represent the remains of service-books from Herefordshire parishes or religious foundations, including Bishops Frome, Kinsham, Ledbury (St Katherine's Hospital), and Leominster (perhaps St Peter's Priory).

While the sparseness of early Hereford sources is probably due largely to the Reformation, earlier losses may also have occurred following revisions of the rite under Sarum influence believed to have been implemented by bishops Trillek and Trefnant, as mentioned. While the nature and extent of these revisions remain uncertain, there are indications that Trefnant, in particular, was interested in liturgy both in its devotional aspects and in terms of reform. An inventory of his books and vestments in his will proved on 23 April 1404[81] includes twelve service-books, consisting of three missals (one specifically said to be of Hereford use bound up with an epistle-book), two graduals (both of Sarum use), a manual, two pontificals, a breviary (*parvum portiforium*), two psalters (one, *psalterium de grossa littera*, probably intended for choir use), and a collectar (*unum collacarium*). A Bible, a legendary (*legenda aurea*), and a commentary on the liturgy (*Rationale divinorum officiorum*) are also recorded. The two Sarum graduals, together with the manual of unspecified use, are significant and may have provided the sources for some of the revisions made to British Library Additional MS 39675 during the late fourteenth or early fifteenth century. Indeed, the graduals, which contained the musical portions for the scriptural elements of the missal (the office, or introit (*antiphona ad introitum*) with its psalm; the gradual, or respond to the epistle; the alleluia with its verse; the offertory (*antiphona ad offertorio*) with its verses following the gospel; and the communion (*antiphona ad communionem*) with its psalm), are very likely to have suggested such revisions. Possession of Sarum books may indicate that Trefnant was exploring ideas and practices beyond those of Hereford use, which may also explain the liturgical commentary in the same list. Its title, *Rationale divinorum officiorum*, identifies it with the famous eight-part treatise of that name by the eminent canonist and liturgist Guillaume Durand, bishop of Mende in southern France (*département* Lozère) from 1286 to 1296.[82] This important and highly influential work, drawing on and developing the ideas of earlier medieval commentators on the liturgy, presents an exposition of Western worship as it had evolved by the mid thirteenth century, allegorically interpreting the sacraments, ceremonies, sacred vessels, vestments, art, architecture, and furnishings of the Church, and elucidating their spiritual significance. It also includes an extensive commentary on burial grounds, together with the various rites of consecration and dedication. The *Rationale* may be seen to stand with the Bible as one of the most frequently copied and widely read texts in medieval Christianity. Trefnant's evident liturgical interests were probably behind any reforms in this direction, both for cathedral and diocese, and it is possible that his visitations of the see conducted in 1397,[83] which revealed considerable deficiencies in statutorily required collections of parochial service-books throughout the diocese, were part of this process. In its moral and disciplinal aspects, too, the diocese was in a similarly questionable state, as indicated by the record of his visitations.

In his introduction to the third volume of the Henry Bradshaw Society edition of *The Hereford Breviary* published in 1915[84] Frere briefly discusses the fourteenth-century revisions of the rite with regard to the breviaries. These revisions also involved the missals as may be seen from the textual variations between them, and in the differences between the ordinary and canon rubrics in two of them (Worcester Cathedral Library MS F.161 and the 1502 printed missal). The evidence suggests that, from the mid fourteenth century, sources for mass and office began to be systematically revised, culminating eventually by way of a presumed series of redacted manuscripts (most of which are now lost) in texts finally represented by the printed service-books, the 1502 missal and the 1505 breviary.[85] This may explain the significant textual variations between the missals, suggesting attempts to upgrade older texts in the light of new, Sarum-based material. In the apparent revisions to Worcester Cathedral Library MS F. 161 the rubrics for the ordinary and canon appear to have been copied, verbatim in places, from the Sarum customary. Substitutions of Sarum prayers throughout the volume, particularly in the sanctorale, are also evident. This may be the text that superseded an earlier source (British Library Additional MS 39675) brought up to date by numerous amendments written over erasures throughout the sanctorale mainly of the offices (introits) with their psalms, the graduals with their verses, the alleluyatic verses, and the offertories and communions possibly by Bishop Trefnant, who seems most likely to have effected this extensive revision. Dating from the late fourteenth or early fifteenth century, these alterations to British Library Additional MS 39675 correspond with the 1502 missal, suggesting the former as an early source-text for this final version. Other attempts to upgrade Additional MS 39675, which in its amended form may have remained at the cathedral until the Reformation, may also account for the removal of the quire between folios 88 and 89 containing most of the Easter Saturday service, together with its prefaces, ordinary and canon. It may have been the intention, though never fulfilled, to replace this quire with another version drawn up in accordance with a Sarum text after the manner of Worcester Cathedral Library MS F. 161. Significantly, this is not the only Hereford manuscript missal with a missing canon, which is also absent from Oxford, University College Library MS 78A. This has lost most of its Easter portion, starting with Maundy Thursday on folio 83v, in addition to the prefaces, ordinary and canon (the last was subsequently replaced with folios 84-6 written on thicker parchment). Possibly, just possibly, originating in the cathedral, this missal was later used in the remote parish church of Whitchurch in the south of the diocese near the Welsh border, where it was adapted for local use by additions to the calendar and propers, in particular those relating to its titular St Dubricius (Dyfrig). The fourth surviving manuscript missal, a small, portable volume,[86] has its canon intact and is associated with St Ethelbert's Hospital formerly by the cathedral, where it probably belonged to the chaplain.

The ordinal[87] and collectar[88] also appear to have belonged to the cathedral, as possibly did the gradual,[89] which, like the noted breviary[90] and one of the missals[91] had later parochial associations. Originating apparently in the cathedral, the breviary migrated from there during the late fifteenth or early sixteenth century to the parish church of Mordiford, about four and a half miles to the south-east of Hereford, where the dedication was added to its calendar under 4 June. The gradual appears to have been owned in turn by two Hereford parishes by the early sixteenth century. Less is known about the little ferial psalter,[92] a beautifully written, personal volume said by Frere to represent Hereford use. The only clue to its early history appears to be a half-erased late fifteenth-century note on an end leaf possibly suggesting northern French ownership at one time.

2 Printed[93]

Printed books representing the Use of Hereford are similarly scarce, consisting of five known copies only of the missal, one in the British Library,[94] three at Oxford,[95] and one in Gloucester Cathedral Library;[96] and two copies, one incomplete, of the 1505 breviary,[97] together with some fragments.[98] Both the missals and the breviary were printed on paper and parchment. The breviary fragments are of parchment and serve as flyleaves to a fourteenth-century Sarum breviary formerly owned by Archbishop Laud – one half of which is now, by a curious turn, in an Australian library – but no complete copy printed on this medium has survived. There are no known books of hours, or, with the exception of two doubtful scraps,[99] processionals. This meagre quantity contrasts significantly with the numerous editions of the Sarum missal and breviary, in addition to a variety of other liturgical texts representing that rite issuing from different European presses for the British market as far afield as Venice between 1475 and 1557, and even later.[100] This notable disparity reflects the widespread dissemination of Sarum use during the later Middle Ages, which resulted in an increasing demand for its books in all their forms. There was also a steady market for books of the York rite, more than those representing Hereford, it must be added, but considerably less than those of Sarum.

The 1505 breviary was printed at Rouen under the patronage of the Lady Margaret Beaufort, countess of Richmond and Derby and Tudor royal matriarch, during the episcopate of Richard Mayhew (1504-

16), and bears her arms on the title-page.[101] Notable is the dedicatory preface by Enghelbert Haghe, the Rouen stationer and publisher responsible for the work, who was also active in London and Hereford during this period. Styling himself conventionally as *cliens* of his patron the Lady Margaret (mentioned forthrightly as *illustrissime viraginis,* 'most illustrious stalwart'),[102] Haghe addresses the Hereford clergy, proclaiming that the service-books (in this case breviary) according to the use of their church mentioned forthrightly as illustrissime viraginis, with great care and expense on the orders (*ad mandata*) of the Lady Margaret, who supported the enterprise. Mention of missals suggests that Haghe may also have had an interest in their production, though the only known edition of the Hereford missal, printed at Rouen in 1502 by Pierre Olivier and Jean Mauditier, was actually published and sold by Jean Richard, another Rouen stationer. The breviaries are described by Haghe as printed (possibly by Olivier and Mauditier) with the best founts and most carefully corrected (*honestissimis caracteribus et summa castigatione*), and due acknowledgement of the cost and industry involved in their production was necessary to ensure the continuing patronage of the Lady Margaret, their generous sponsor. The absence of a printed folio choir breviary to complement the 1502 missal is notable and may suggest that there was a limit to the Lady Margaret's generosity. It is possible that her patronage had extended earlier to contributing to the costs of the missal, but there is so far no evidence of this.

---

57. Ibid., Smith, *Use of Hereford*, Ch. 4, *The sources*, I Manuscript.
58. Hereford Cathedral Library MS P. i. 2.
59. Cambridge, Pembroke College Library MS 302.
60. *ASC* C 1055 (*þæt hig beryptan 7 bereafodan æt haligdome 7 æt hreaue 7 æt eallon ðingan*), see also *supra* note 22.
61. Hereford Cathedral Library MS O. ix. 2.
62. Hereford Cathedral Library MS O. i. 8.
63. Hereford Cathedral Library MS P. vii. 6.
64. Hereford Cathedral Library MS P. viii. 7.
65. Hereford Cathedral Library MS P. ix. 7, fol. i; Oxford, Bodleian Library MS Hatton 106, fol. i.

66. London, University of London, Senate House Library MS 639/1, as end leaf (previously pastedown) to a printed book, 1498.

67. Hereford Cathedral Library MS P. ix. 7.

68. London, British Library Harley MS 2983, fols. 47-82v.

69. Hereford Cathedral Library MS H. vii. 9, previously upper pastedown to a printed book, 1554.

70. Hereford Cathedral Library MS P. vii. 1.

71. London, British Library Additional MS 39675.

72. Oxford, University College Library MS 78A; Worcester Cathedral Library MS F.161; Stratton-on-the-Fosse, Downside Abbey Library MS 48243.

73. MS privately owned (cited by Smith, *Use of Hereford*, 254, 309-12, as the 'Benson Psalter') consisting of a breviary portion, fols. 118-143v, with earlier (1262 x c.1300?) non-liturgical psalter, fols. 5-88v; Worcester Cathedral Library MS Q. 86; United States, Los Angeles, University of California, C. E. Young Research Library MS Rouse 97.

74. London, British Library Harley MS 2983, fols. 1-21, 22-46, *s.*xiv *in.*

75. London, British Library Harley MS 3965, *s.*xiv (last quarter).

76. Oxford, Balliol College Library MS 321, *s.*xiii *ex*/xiv *in.*

77. Oxford, University College Library MS 7, *s.*xiv *ex*/xv *in.*; Oxford, Bodleian Library Lat. liturg. e. 48 (with London and Oxford as well as Hereford associations), *s.*xv *med.*

78. Oxford, Bodleian Library MS Rawlinson B. 328, *s.*xiv *med.*

79. Oxford, Bodleian Library MS Laud misc. 681, fols. 5-10v, *s.*xv *med.*

80. Hereford Cathedral Archives MS Cap. 41/1, *s.*xiv.

81. Hereford Cathedral Archives MS 2126.

82. *The Rationale Divinorum Officiorum of William Durand of Mende, a new translation of the Prologue and Book One*, by Timothy M. Thibodeau, Records of Western Civilization Series, Columbia University Press, 2010. Books Two (*On the Ministers and the Ecclesiastical Orders and their Offices*) and Three (*On the Vestments of the Priests, Bishops and Other Ministers*), also translated by Thibodeau, were published together as *William Durand on the Clergy and their Vestments* (Pennsylvania: University of Scranton Press (distributed by University of Chicago Press), 2010).

83. Smith, *Use of Hereford*, Appendix I, *Surviving and untraced liturgica*, (iii) The diocese of Hereford in 1397.

84. Frere and Brown, *The Hereford Breviary* (see Bibliography 1).

85. For the missal, see Henderson, *Missale ad usum percelebris ecclesiae Herfordensis*, 1874 (Bibliography 1).

86. Stratton-on-the-Fosse, Downside Abbey Library MS 48243.

87. London, British Library Harley MS 2983.

88. Oxford, Balliol College Library MS 321.

89. London, British Library Harley MS 3965.

90. Hereford Cathedral Library MS P. ix. 7.

91. Oxford, University College Library MS 78A.

92. Oxford, University College Library MS 7.

93. Smith, *Use of Hereford*, Ch. 4, *The sources*, II *Printed*.

94. London, British Library C. 35. i. 4, which was sold to the British Museum (later British Library) for £300 by the ecclesiastical antiquary William Maskell (for whom, see J. M. Rigg (revised by David Maskell), 'Maskell, William (1814-1890), Roman Catholic convert and liturgical scholar', *ODNB*. https://doi.org/10.1093/ref:odnb/18265) in 1858 (Smith, *Use of Hereford*, Ch. 4, *The sourc-*

es, II *Printed/Missals*, 356). Maskell had somehow acquired this book from the Trenchard Street Friary of the Bristol Franciscans serving the Roman Catholic chapel of St Mary on the Quay in the city centre.

95. Bodleian Library Arch B. c. 6, Vet. E1. c. 11, and St John's College b. 2. 2. The first belonged at one time to Thomas Hearne (c.1678–1735), the Oxford antiquary (for whom, see Theodor Harmsen, 'Hearne, Thomas (bap. 1678, d. 1735), antiquary and diarist', *ODNB*. https://doi.org/10.1093/ref:oxforddnb/12827), passing after his death to Richard Rawlinson, who bequeathed it to the Bodleian together with other books in 1755 (Smith, *Use of Hereford*, Ch. 4, *The sources*, II *Printed/ Missals*, 358). This is classed as a Bodleian Library Select Volume requiring special permission to examine it.

96. Gloucester Cathedral Library 252.

97. Worcester Cathedral Library SEL. A. 50. 3; Oxford, Bodleian Library Gough Missals 69, with offices for half the year (*pars aestivalis*) only.

98. Oxford, Bodleian Library Laud misc. MS 3A, fols. 1–2, 204–5.

99. Oxford, Christ Church College Library f. 9. 12, as paper flyleaves to a printed book of 1541 belonging formerly to Robert Burton (for whom, see J. B. Bamborough, 'Burton, Robert (1577–1640), writer', *ODNB*. http://www.oxfordddnb.com/view/article/4137). Burton, who remained at Christ Church until his death in 1640, becoming librarian in 1624, is best remembered for his *Anatomy of Melancholy* first published in 1621.

100. A number of Sarum books, in particular missals, breviaries and *horae*, continued to be printed for a while on the Continent to meet the needs of English Catholic Recusants abroad after the death of Queen Mary on 17 November 1558.

101. Smith, *Use of Hereford*, Ch. 4, *The sources*, II *Printed/Breviaries*, 366-71 (Worcester Cathedral Library SEL. A. 50. 3), 372-4 (Oxford, Bodleian Library Gough Missals 69).

102. Ibid., read Smith, *Use of Hereford*, Ch. 4, *The sources*, II *Printed/Breviaries*, 369.

5

The distinctiveness of the Use of Hereford

The surviving missals, breviaries and other Hereford service-books offer a glimpse, albeit perplexing and inconclusive, into a far from tidy process of liturgical development, which apparently took place under increasing Sarum influence at a time of similar encroachments on other British diocesan rites. Frere has indicated that both the ordinal and the 1505 printed breviary show considerable signs of borrowing from Sarum sources, with sections of their rubrics copied directly from the old and new forms of the ordinal as well as the customary. The full extent of this plagiarization, however, is difficult to assess, for 'if we attempt to examine the matter more minutely, we shall find it hard to arrive at any clear-cut results'.[104] Frere's remarks apply no less to the missals, which form the principal subject of the author's study, and which similarly display evidence of Sarum borrowing, particularly in the propers, the collects, secrets and postcommunions. Like the breviary office collects, which derive from the collectar and the missals, these also illustrate, if only partially, the same process of assimilation to Sarum. This is supported by further comparisons of the ordinaries and canons of Worcester Cathedral Library MS F. 161 and the 1502 printed missal with the Sarum customary, as has been attempted in Chapter 7 of the author's book. Analyses have also been made of the sequences,[105] the post-Pentecost alleluyatic verses,[106] the pre- and post-canon prayers,[107] and the calendar and litany[108] allowing a wider overview of the evidently complex inter-relationship between the various sources involved. Had more material been available, it might have been possible to answer further questions, and to make more definite assumptions about the putative influences on the surviving missals and breviaries, as well as the sources underlying them, but this has not been possible. It would have been of considerable interest, for example, to know what, if any, were the manuscript exemplars for the 1502 missal and the 1505 breviary,[109] the source-texts on which these single editions were based, and how and by what means these were made available to the northern French (Rouen) printers concerned with their production, questions probably never likely to be answered in the light of the sparse existing evidence.

This process of gradual adoption and assimilation, however, never altered the essential character of the liturgy of the church of Hereford, which made it a distinctive liturgical 'use', and which enabled it to maintain its independence against Sarum throughout the Middle Ages. Its distinguishing features include the cathedral's *festa loci sancti*, in particular those of its two most important saints, Ethelbert and Thomas Cantilupe, separated by nearly five centuries, and also the individuality of its ancient customs (*consuetudines*) contributing to the uniqueness of that 'use'. Apart from the Holy Week ceremonial famously described by Edmund Bishop, other notable characteristics of the rite include the offering of the eucharistic bread and wine together with a single prayer; a third ablution of the chalice with water only; the laying of the chalice horizontally on the paten after completion of mass; the absence of a blessing or final gospel to indicate the end of mass; the recital of the Lenten preface *Qui corporali ieiunio* at every mass from Ash Wednesday (*de ieiunio*) to Palm Sunday (*ad ramos palmarum*), with the injunctions *Flectamus genua, Levate,* and *Humiliate capita vestra deo* on week days (*in feriis*) up until Maundy Thursday (*feria v in die cene, cena domini*) except on Ember Saturday (not classed as a ferial day) during Lent (*Sabbato quatuor temporum*);[110] and the discontinuation of prostrations at mass from Advent between the *Sanctus* and the beginning of the communion prayer until after the feast of the Purification of the Blessed Virgin (2 February) or Septuagesima, whichever came first. The series of offertory verses for Sundays in Septuagesima and Sexagesima, and for Ash Wednesday (*feria iv in capite ieiunii*) with Thursday and Friday of that week (*feria v, feria vi post cineres*) seems to have been a peculiarity of the later Hereford rite, since it is absent from the manuscript missals and the gradual. Also significant was the singing of the hymn *Veni creator* by the celebrant during the Ablution (hand washing) after the first of the pre-canon prayers, *Suscipe sancte trinitas*,[111] a practice not followed by the Sarum rite. On completion of *Suscipe sancte trinitas* at Hereford, the celebrant put down the chalice (*reponat calicem*) containing wine and water held during the prayer, covering it with corporals (*cum corporalibus*), before which he carefully (*decenter*) placed the paten with the bread also on corporals. He then kissed the paten and moved it to the right-hand side of the altar, partly covering it (*parum cooperiendo*) with corporals, before proceeding to the Ablution[112] with *Veni creator* and its verse *Emitte spiritum tuum et creabuntur, et renovabis faciem terre.* The second pre-canon prayer, *Ure igni sancti spiritus*,[113] apparently unique to Hereford, was then commenced. In the York rite the celebrant recited (*dicat*) *Lavabo inter innocentes manus meas et circumdabo altare tuum, domine* [Psalm 25, v. 6] during this Ablution followed by *Veni creator*.[114] At Hereford the *Lavabo* with an optional additional verse (*ut audiam vocem laudis, ut enarrem uniuersa mirabilia tua*) was said (*dicat*) during the final Ablution at the piscina (*sacrarium*),[115] immediately before the communion and postcommunion prayers, followed by *Dominus uobiscum* with its choir response *Et cum spiritu tuo* according to the earlier form of the rite.[116]

Vestments were also an integral and distinctive part of the Hereford liturgical identity. The blessing of water before mass was conducted by a priest (*sacerdos*) in alb and amice (*alba et amictu*), while at Salisbury a red cope was worn for the occasion. The colour of the silk cope in the York rite here is uncertain. At Hereford chasubles were prescribed for the deacon and subdeacon at mass during the Sundays of Advent through to Septuagesima and Lent up to Easter. On ferial days (*in feriis*), both during this period and from Trinity to Advent as well as for vigils, Ember Days (*dies ieiunii*), certain votives (*pro Familiaribus, de Cruce*) and masses for the dead, and anniversaries of kings, bishops and patrons, albs were worn. The dalmatic and tunicle (*dalmatica et tunica*) were ordered for Ember Days during Whitsun, and on Maundy Thursday. The practice of wearing albs on ferial days appears to have been a peculiarity of the York rite also. At Salisbury, Exeter and Wells chasubles were directed for those days as well as Sundays.

During the mass of the chrism on Maundy Thursday following the *Sanctus* three deacons in amices with silk palls carried the chrismatory (*ampulla chrismatis*) with the holy oils (*liquores*) for consecration beneath a tabernacle (*tabernaculum*) supported by four priest-vicars (*sacerdotes vicarii*) in albs and chasubles. Heading the procession were three acolytes (*tres pueri acolythi*) with cross, candle (*cereo*) and thrurible (*thuribulo*) accompanied by two canons (*duo canonici*) singing the antiphon *O redemptor*. The oils were then offered to the bishop by the canons for consecration at the high altar, after which the tabernacle and chrism returned to the sanctuary following the same order of procession, while the canons sang the antiphon *Ut novetur*. The oil of the catechumens was now ready for the baptisms that traditionally took place at the Easter vigil. During mass on this day neither the Pax (*Pax domini*) was given nor *Agnus dei* said, the celebrating bishop or priest kissing the chrismatory or chalice in place of the customary kiss of peace.

Albs and red chasubles (*albis et casulis rubeis*), and black silk copes (*capis nigris de serico*) were worn by four priests (*quatuor presbiteri*) in pairs singing the responsories and versicles during the ritual of the Cross on Good Friday. Lenten vestments (*vestibus quadragesimalibus*), as they are described in the missal rubric without indication of colour, were ordered for the ministers (*ministris*) assisting the bishop on this day, all of whom, according to the later (1502) form of the Hereford rite, proceeded discalced (*nudibus pedibus*) to the high altar. When the bishop was installed in his usual place by the high altar (*more solito iuxta altare*), the reading of the lessons with tracts commenced followed by the Passion from St John's Gospel with genuflections, and responsories and versicles preceding the veneration of the Cross. During the Easter vigil the bishop received a chasuble (*accepta casula*) to put on before beginning the *Kyrie eleyson* as a prelude to the mass of the catechumens on the cantors' order *Accendite* to light all the candles throughout the church after the singing of the litany by three clerks of the third rank (*tres clerici tercie forme*). The ringing of the church bells (*tunc omnes campane pulsentur*) then signalled the start of mass, with collect *Deus qui sacratissimam noctem*. After the epistle two canons in silk copes (*capis sericis*) sang in high voice (*alta voce*) the psalm *Confitemini domino* with preceding *Alleluia*. The following rubric directed all wearing black copes (*capas nigras*) to lay them down during the *Alleluia*, but resume them again afterwards. Two priest-vicars in black copes then sang the tract *Laudate dominum* preceding the gospel. During the Ascension Day procession two priests in amices, with heads covered and bowed (*capitibus opertis, dimissis in terra vultibus*) and holding palms, sang in low voice (*humili voce*) the responsories *Viri Galilei* and *Quemadmodum*. On the feast of All Souls (*Commemoratio animarum*) on 2 November a black samite cope (*capa de nigra samita*) was worn by the celebrant (*executor officii*) as befitted the solemnity of the occasion.

Hereford's uniqueness as a *locus sanctus* was thus inseparable from its characteristic 'use' as represented by its distinctive liturgy (which comprised its feasts, ritual, vestments and sacred music), customs and architecture, each contributing in its own way to this individuality. The influence of Sarum on its service-books, most particularly the missals and breviaries, did little to diminish this distinctiveness, which enabled Hereford use to continue as of old up until the reign of Elizabeth I, when it was finally abolished by the statutory imposition of the revised *Book of Common Prayer* in 1559. Marking the end of the ancient Latin liturgy in England, this began a new era of national corporate worship with the vernacular as the language of devotion, with its stately resonances, like those of the King James Bible, sounding down the ages as a rich and living part of our spiritual and literary heritage. From the mid fourteenth century Sarum influences were gradually assimilated to become an intrinsic part of the evolving Hereford use, complementing and enhancing rather than altering its essential character. No mere plagiarists, the compilers of its later service-books, apparently beginning during Trillek's episcopate and continuing through Trefnant's up until the beginning of the sixteenth century, evidently distinguished between creative borrowing and unquestioning imitation in their selection of sources, as suggested by the famous rubric in the 1505 breviary regulating the weekly office lessons up to Advent. Beginning *Nec omnino ut fingunt Sarisburienses*, 'Not entirely as they do at Salisbury', this served as a timely reminder to all that the Use of Hereford was, and continued to be, distinctive as one of the principal diocesan liturgies of medieval England without compromising its unique character, and existing on no other terms but its own despite its evident indebtedness to Sarum during the later Middle Ages.

---

103. Ibid., Ch. 17, *Conclusion:* 'Not entirely as they do at Salisbury', on which this section is largely based.

104. Frere, *Use of Hereford* 3, xliii-xliv.

105. Smith, *Use of Hereford*, Ch. 10, *The sequences.*

106. Ibid., Ch. 11, *The invariable portions of the missal:* 1 *The alleluyatic verses for Sundays following Trinity, or the octaves of Pentecost.*

107. Ibid., Ch. 11, *The invariable portions of the missal:* 2 *The pre- and post-canon prayers.*

108. Ibid., Ch. 12, *The calendar and litany.*

109. The late fourteenth- or early fifteenth-century sanctorale amendments (mainly of the offices (introits) with their psalms, the graduals with their verses, the alleluyatic verses, and the offertories and communions) to British Library Additional MS 39675 have been tentatively suggested by the writer as possible source-texts for by the writer as possible source-texts for these portions of the 1502 missal.

110. The rubric in the 1502 missal does not indicate precisely when these injunctions occur in the ferial day services, simply ordering that '... *Flectamus genua, Levate,* et *Humiliate capita vestra deo* dicuntur quotidie in feriis usque ad cenam domini excepto Sabbato quatuor temporum', though the context may suggest that these preceded the Lenten preface *Qui corporali ieiunio* (Henderson (ed.), *Missale ad usum percelebris ecclesiae Herfordensis* (1874), 42).

111. This prayer appears to be of northern Frankish origin and probably dates from the late eighth century, when it starts to become widespread (Smith, *Use of Hereford*, 558, note 20). Besides Hereford, it occurs here with variations in the Sarum and York rites as well as in those of Rouen, Bayeux and Paris, and Nidaros (Trondheim, Norway), among others, and earlier in some of the Carolingian sacramentaries (ibid.). In the *Micrologus*, an eleventh-century treatise on the Roman liturgy of the mass and the liturgical year attributed to Bernold of Constance (c.1054-1100), monk of the Black Forest abbey of St Blasien near Schaffhausen, *Suscipe sancte trinitas* is preceded by *Veni sanctificator* (*PL* 151, 973-1022, at 984, lines 1-7). Originally a Gallican offertory prayer, *Veni sanctificator* is found in the Hereford rite as the last of the pre-canon prayers immediately before the signing of the chalice, *Bene + dic et sanctifica hoc sacrificium* (Smith, *Use of Hereford*, 404, 406, 559 with notes 23, 25).

112. Like the final Ablution, this presumably took place at the piscina (*sacrarium*), though this is not mentioned here, the rubric in the 1502 missal merely directing that 'Et postea eat [sacerdos] ad abluendum manus suas, et in eundo dicat totum hymnum *Veni creator*, excepto uersu *Dudum sacrata*, cum uersu *Emitte spiritum tuum*' (Smith, *Use of Hereford*, 404-5). The use of *dicat* in both Ablution rubrics seems to be equivalent to *canat*.

113. Smith, *Use of Hereford*, 404-5.

114. Ibid., 558-9.

115. Ibid., 408-9, 561.

116. As represented by Worcester Cathedral Library MS F.161, fol. 101r (Smith, *Use of Hereford*, 409). In the 1502 missal *Dominus uobiscum* preceded the postcommunion (ibid.), which was followed by *Per dominum nostrum iesum christum filium tuum. Qui tecum uiuit ...* and the concluding *Dominus uobiscum* and *Ite missa est* (Smith, *Use of Hereford*, 409).

6

Epilogue

It may be asked why the Use of Hereford was never superseded by the Use of Sarum as in other British cathedrals, such as London, Lincoln, Chichester, Wells, Exeter, Lichfield, St Davids, and Glasgow, where liturgical reforms were implemented in parallel with capitular reorganization initiated by the adoption of Sarum customs from the late twelfth century. The answer to this anomaly may lie in the variation in constitutional evolution between the different foundations, with Hereford, like York, displaying an apparent independence of Sarum influence on its early statutes, as has been noted. Significantly, these were the two foundations that preserved the integrity of their individual rites, Hereford albeit to a lesser degree than York, until the mid sixteenth century. The Hereford *Consuetudines*,[117] or collection of cathedral customs, which are believed to have been formulated under the initiative of Bishop Peter of Aigueblanche, represent this independence. The putative reforms of this period attributed to Aigueblanche appear to have been part of a wider process of transformation intended to create Hereford's unique constitutional and liturgical identity, an identity that was to endure until well beyond the Reformation. This distinctiveness later found expression in the publication of its two principal service-books at the beginning of the sixteenth century, the 1502 missal and the 1505 breviary. Both were presumably the result of collaboration between the bishop, who would have required these books for the diocese, and the dean and chapter concerned primarily with the performance of the cathedral liturgy. Who was around then to ensure their production and dissemination? The bishop at the time of publication of the missal was Adriano da Castello (Castellesi)[118] and the dean apparently Reginald West, who was known to be in office by 1503, perhaps succeeding John Hervey shortly after February 1501. The Italian Castello was appointed bishop by Henry VII on 14 February 1502, less than seven months before the missal was printed at Rouen on 1 September that year, being translated (probably on his own insistence) to the more lucrative see of Bath and Wells on 2 August 1504. Given his unscrupulous and self-interested character (earlier in his career he had tried to purchase for himself the office of cardinal), however, and the fact that he resided in neither see during his episcopates, it strains credibility to suppose that Hereford's liturgical or pastoral concerns were uppermost in his mind. Castello's apparent lack of interest in his church and diocese may suggest that West and his chapter were solely responsible for commissioning the missal in the first instance for the cathedral previous to extending it for diocesan use in eventual collaboration with the bishop. A more likely person to have initiated the missal would have been Castello's predecessor Edmund Audley, who was bishop from 1492 until his translation to Salisbury on 10 January 1502, just over a month before his successor's appointment. The missal's title on its first leaf (sig. [Ai]) indicates that it had been printed by authority of both the bishop, and the dean and chapter,[119] but which bishop and dean are not named.

After twenty-two years at Salisbury Audley died on 23 August 1524. A conscientious and conservative bishop of the old school, he is remembered for his piety and the fine chantry chapels he founded in both Hereford and Salisbury cathedrals.[120] Less pleasant to recall is his reputation as a determined persecutor of Lollards throughout his diocese, with regular burnings of relapsed heretics between 1502 and 1520. It is of interest to note that Hereford Cathedral Library possesses a

Lollard, or Wycliffite version of the Bible dating from the early fifteenth century.[121] Its medieval provenance is uncertain, but it is known to have been given to the cathedral by Robert Bennet, who was bishop from 1603 to 1617. Its liturgical interest lies in its initial leaves, which are part of a folio Sarum *kalendarium*, unusually in English (March-December only), with incipits and explicits of the lessons for each feast, also in English. If this book originated at Hereford, it is tempting to imagine that it may have passed through Audley's hands during his episcopate before its eventual acquisition by Bennet, though this can only be surmised, as is Audley's possible involvement in the authorization and promulgation of the printed missal. In any event, both the Hereford missal and breviary are what nowadays would be termed 'one-offs', since neither was reprinted, perhaps because of expense and limited demand. It may be that the missal originated through episcopal mandate in the manner, for example, of the Norwegian Nidaros (Trondheim) missal and breviary commissioned and subsidized by Archbishop Erik Walkendorf, and both published in 1519,[122] but there is no indication of this. Their existence, however, is clear evidence that the Use of Hereford continued to maintain its independence in a Province largely dominated by Sarum until the mid sixteenth century. One imagines how it might have evolved further had it not been for the Reformation (would the missal and breviary have been revised and reprinted, for example, and by whom?), but then our story is full of tantalizing 'what ifs', which may never be answered in the light of our present knowledge, if at all. Suffice it to say for now that the Use of Hereford will continue to be remembered as one of the principal diocesan liturgies of medieval England, which makes it so very distinctive.

---

117. Hereford Cathedral Archives MS 7044/1.

118. T. F. Mayer, 'Castellesi [da Castello, da Corneto], Adriano (c.1461–1521), cardinal and English agent in Rome', *ODNB*. http://www.oxforddnb.com/view/article/174.

119. '... hoc nouum et egregium opus sacri Missalis ad vsum famose ac percelebris ecclesie / Hel-

forden*sis*. nuper instanti ac peruigili cura visum correctum et emendatum. / Necno*n* auctoritate reuerendi in christo patris et d*omi*ni eiusdem ecclesie epyscopi / meritissimi ... ac domi*norum* decani et capituli ...' [Expansions and rubricated portions of text are represented by italics and underlining respectively].

120. G. H. Cook, *Mediaeval Chantries and Chantry Chapels* (London: Phoenix House, 1947), 46, 65, 107, 119 (with illustration (Plate 26) of the Salisbury chantry); C. Oakes, 'In pursuit of heaven: the two chantry chapels of Bishop Edmund Audley at Hereford and Salisbury cathedrals', *Journal of the British Archaeological Association* 164 (2011), Issue 1 (*The Medieval Chantry in England*), 196–220. For Audley, who was buried in his Salisbury chantry, see Jonathan Hughes, 'Audley, Edmund (c.1439–1524), bishop of Salisbury', *ODNB*. http://www. oxforddnb.com/view/article/891.

121. Hereford Cathedral Library MS O. vii. 1.

122. The title-page of the breviary (dated 4 July 1519), which followed the missal, begins *Breuiaria ad vsum ritumque sacrosancte Nidrosiensis Ecclesie. Iam primum solerti optimorum artificum diligentia : impensis vero ac mandatis insignibus longe reuerendi in christo patris et domini : domini Erici Walkendorff eiusdem ecclesie archiepiscopi dignissimi felix faustumque accipiunt exordium* (Paris: Jean Kerbriant *alias* Huguelin & Jean Bienayse, 1519, in-8o): facsimile reproduction, 2 vols. (1 Liturgical Survey, 2 Bibliographical Survey), ed. H. Buvarp and B. M. Børsum (Oslo: Børsums forlag og antikvariat, 1964). The Nidaros missal (facsimile reproduction, Oslo, Børsums forlag og antikvariat, 1959), printed in Copenhagen and dated 25 May 1519 (Paulus Reff, in-folio), was also initiated by the Danish Walkendorf, who was (penultimate Roman Catholic) archbishop of Nidaros from 1510 to 1522 (Lars Hamre, *Erik Valkendorf, Trekk av hans liv og virke* (Bergen: John Griegs Forlag, 1943), 54-67). Both the breviary and the missal are discussed by Lilli Gjerløw, 'The Breviarium and the Missale Nidrosiense (1519)', in Hans Bekker-Nielsen, Marianne Børch and Bengt Algot Sørensen (eds.), From *Script to Book*, Proceedings of the Seventh International Symposium, Centre for the Study of Vernacular Literature in the Middle Ages, held at Odense University, 15–16 November 1982, Odense University Press (1982), 50–77, 168–9. See also Smith, *Use of Hereford*, Ch. 1, *Introduction*, 7, with n. 35, and ibid., *Bibliography*, at 739, 761.

Select Bibliography

1 *Liturgical, mainly Hereford and Sarum rites*

Abercrombie, N., *The Life and Work of Edmund Bishop*, with Foreword by D. M. Knowles (London: Longmans, Green & Co. Ltd, 1959).

Bishop, E., *Liturgica Historica, Papers on the Liturgy and Religious Life of the Western Church*, ed. R. H. Connolly and K. Sisam (Oxford: Clarendon Press, 1918).

Cummings, B., *The Book of Common Prayer, the Texts of 1549, 1559 and 1662*, with introduction and notes (Oxford: Oxford University Press, 2011).

Dickinson, F. H., *List of Printed Service Books according to the Ancient Uses of the Anglican Church* (London: Joseph Masters, 1850).

Frère, E. B., *Des livres de liturgie des églises d'Angleterre (Salisbury, York, Hereford) imprimés à Rouen dans les xve et xvie siècles* (Rouen : Le Brument, 1867).

Frere, W. H., *The Use of Sarum, the Original Texts edited from the MSS*, with introduction and index, 2 vols. (Cambridge: Cambridge University Press, 1898, 1901): 1 *Sarum Customs as set forth in the Consuetudinary and Customary*, 2 Ordinal and Tonal.

Frere W. H., and Brown, L. E. G. (eds.), *The Hereford Breviary*, 3 vols., London: Henry Bradshaw Society 26 (1904), 40 (1911), 46 (1915) [edited from *Breuiarium secundum vsum herford'* (Rouen, 7 July 1505, in-8o) and manuscript sources, in particular Hereford Cathedral Library MS P. ix. 7, the thirteenth-century noted Hereford breviary].

Henderson, W. G. (ed.), *Missale ad usum percelebris ecclesiae Herfordensis* (Leeds: M'Corquodale & Co. Ltd, 1874) [edited from *Missale ad vsum famose ac percelebris ecclesie helforden'* (Rouen: Pierre Olivier & Jean Mauditier, 1 September 1502, in-folio) and Oxford, University College Library MS 78A], reprinted by Gregg International Publishers Ltd, Farnborough (Hampshire, UK), 1969, and Kessinger Publishing, Whitefish (Montana, USA), 2008.

A. Hughes, *Medieval Manuscripts for Mass and Office, A Guide to their Organization and Terminology* (Toronto, Buffalo & London: University of Toronto Press, 1982, reprinted 1986, and 1995 with addenda).

King, A. A., *Liturgies of the Past* (London: Longmans, Green & Co. Ltd, 1959).

Klauser, T., *A Short History of the Western Liturgy, An Account and some Reflections*, translated from the German by John Halliburton (London, New York and Toronto: Oxford University Press, 1969).

Levien, E., 'On the Hereford Missal', *Journal of the British Archaeological Association* 27 (1871), 424-9.

Maskell, W., *The Ancient Liturgy of the Church of England*, 3rd edn. (Oxford: Clarendon Press, 1882).

Maskell, W., *Monumenta Ritualia Ecclesiae Anglicanae, or, Occasional Offices of the Church of England according to the Ancient Use of Salisbury, the Prymer in English, and other Prayers and Forms, with dissertations and notes*, 2nd edn., 3 vols. (Oxford: Clarendon Press, 1882).

Pfaff, R. W., *The Liturgy in Medieval England, A History* (Cambridge: Cambridge University Press, 2009).

Procter, F., and Frere, W. H., *A New History of the Book of Common Prayer, with a Rationale of its Offices*, 3rd edn. (London: Macmillan & Co., 1907).

Sandon, N. (ed.), *The Use of Salisbury*, 6 vols. (Newton Abbot and Moretonhampstead: Antico Edition Liturgical Church Music, 1984-99): 1 *The Ordinary of the Mass* (1984, 2nd edn. 1990), 2 *The Proper of the Mass in Advent*, 3 *The Proper of the Mass from Septuagesima to Palm Sunday*, 4 *Masses and Ceremonies of Holy Week*, 5 *The Proper of the Mass from Easter to Trinity*, 6 *The Proper of the Mass from Trinity to Advent* [Proper chants, with prayers, readings and rubrics for the Salisbury liturgical year].

Sandon, N., 'Salisbury ['Sarum'], Use of', in S. Sadie and J. Tyrrell (eds.), *The New Grove Dictionary of Music and Musicians*, 2nd revised edn., 29 vols. (Oxford: Oxford University Press, 2004): 22, 158-63 (https://doi.org/10.1093/gmo/9781561592630.article.24611).

Sheppard, L. C., 'Rites, English Medieval', in *New Catholic Encyclopedia*, 14 vols. with index (New York: McGraw Hill, 1967, with four supplements, 1972, 1978, 1988, and 1995; 2nd edn. 2002): 10, 519b-522b.

Smith, W., *The Use of Hereford, The Sources of a Medieval English Diocesan Rite* (Farnham, Surrey: Ashgate Publishing Ltd, 2015, from 2017 published by Routledge), ISBN 9781472412775 (hardback), ISBN 9781472412782 (e-book and PDF).

Teviotdale, E. C., *The Cotton Troper* ([*London*] *British Library, Cotton MS Caligula A.xiv, ff. 1-36: A Study of an Illustrated English Troper of the Eleventh Century*), University of North Carolina, Chapel Hill, unpublished PhD thesis, 1992.

Teviotdale, E. C., 'Some thoughts on the place of origin of the Cotton Troper', in László Dobszay (ed.), *Cantus Planus: Papers Read at the Fourth Meeting* (Budapest: Hungarian Academy of Sciences, 1992), 407-12.

Teviotdale, E. C., "The Hereford Troper' and Hereford', in D. Whitehead (ed.), *Medieval Art, Architecture and Archaeology at Hereford, British Archaeological Association Conference Transactions* 15 (1995), 75-81.

Teviotdale, E. C., '[Cambridge] Pembroke College [MS] 302: Abbreviated Gospel Book or Gospel Lectionary?', in G. H. Brown and L. E. Voigts (eds.), *The Study of Medieval Manuscripts of England: Festschrift in Honor of Richard W. Pfaff*, Arizona Studies in the Middle Ages and the Renaissance 35, Medieval and Renaissance Texts and Studies 384

(Tempe, Arizona: Arizona Center for Medieval and Renaissance Studies in collaboration with Brepols Publishers, Turnhout, 2010), 69-99.

Wordsworth, C., and Littlehales, H., *The Old Service-Books of the English Church*, The Antiquary's Books (London: Methuen & Co. Ltd, 1904).

2 *The cults of St Ethelbert and St Thomas Cantilupe*

Alington, G., *St Thomas Cantilupe*, with illustrations by Dominic Harbour (Leominster: Gracewing, 2001).

Bannister, A. T., 'The Hereford miracles', *Transactions of the Woolhope Naturalists' Field Club*, unnumbered volume issued September 1905 for the years 1902, 1903 and 1904, 377-83.

Brooks, B. C. (ed.), *The Life of St Ethelbert, King and Martyr, 779-794: East Saxon king of East Anglia, son of Ethelred, eleventh linear descendant after Rædwald* (Bury St Edmunds: Bury Clerical Society, 1995).

Caldwell, J., 'St Ethelbert, King and Martyr, his cult and office in the West of England', *Plainsong and Medieval Music* 1, pt. 10 (Cambridge: Cambridge University Press, April 2000), 39-46.

Dewick, E. S., 'On some Masses of St Ethelbert, K.[King] [and] M.[Martyr], in a Manuscript Missal of Hereford Use', *Transactions of the St Paul's Ecclesiological Society* 4 (1900), 235-6.

Emmerson, R., 'St Thomas Cantilupe's tomb and brass of 1287', *Bulletin of the International Society for the Study of Church Monuments* 2 (1980), 41-5.

Farmer, D. H., *The Oxford Dictionary of Saints*, Oxford Paperback Reference, 5th revised edn. (Oxford: Oxford University Press, 2003, reissued 2011), 178b-179a (art. 'Ethelbert (2) (779-94), king of the East Angles') and 507a-508b (art. 'Thomas of Hereford (Thomas Cantelupe) (1218-82), bishop').

Finucane, R. C., *Miracles and Pilgrims, Popular Beliefs in Medieval England* (London: J. M. Dent & Sons Ltd, 1977, reprinted in paperback, New York: St Martin's Press, 1995).

Greaves, M., 'Anglicans venerate relic of medieval English saint', *Catholic Herald* 6379 (14 November 2008), 3.

Horne, Dom E., OSB, 'The head of St Thomas of Hereford', *Clergy Review*, New Series 28 (1947), 99-104.

James, M. R. (ed.), 'Two lives of St Ethelbert, King and Martyr', *English Historical Review* 32 (1917), 214-44.

Jancey, M. (ed.), *St Thomas Cantilupe, Bishop of Hereford: Essays in his Honour* (Hereford: Friends of Hereford Cathedral Publications Committee for the Dean and Chapter, 1982).

Jancey, M., St Ethelbert, *Patron Saint of Hereford Cathedral* (Hereford: Friends of

Hereford Cathedral, 1994).

Marshall, G., 'The shrine of St Thomas de Cantilupe in Hereford Cathedral', *Transactions of the Woolhope Naturalists' Field Club* 27 (1930-2), 34-50.

Morris, J., SJ, 'English relics: 1 St Thomas of Hereford', *The Month, A Catholic Magazine and Review* 44 (January-April 1882), 112-26.

Nilson, B., *Cathedral Shrines of Medieval England* (Woodbridge: Boydell Press, 1998, 2nd edition, 2001).

Rollason, D. W., *Saints and Relics in Anglo-Saxon England* (Oxford: Basil Blackwell, 1989).

Rollason, D. W., 'St Æthelberht of Hereford and the cults of European royal saints', *Cantilupe Journal* 18 (2008), 8-26.

Ross, J. H., and Jancey, M., 'The miracles of St Thomas of Hereford', *British Medical Journal* (Clinical Research Edition) 295 (6613), 19-26 December 1987, 1590-4 (http://www.ncbi. nlm.nih.gov/pmc/articles/PMC1257483).

Stubbs, C. W., 'The Hereford miracles', *Transactions of the Woolhope Naturalists' Field Club* 18 (1902-4), 377-83.

Tavinor, M., *Shrines of the Saints in England and Wales*, with Foreword by Sir Roy Strong (Norwich: Canterbury Press (an imprint of Hymns Ancient and Modern Ltd), 2016).

3 *General, mainly Hereford Cathedral and the history of the diocese*

Aylmer, G. E., and Tiller, J. (eds.), *Hereford Cathedral, A History* (London and Rio Grande: The Hambledon Press, 2000).

Bannister, A. T., *The Cathedral Church of Hereford, its History and Constitution* (London: SPCK, 1924).

Bannister, A. T., 'Visitation returns of the diocese of Hereford in 1397', *English Historical Review* 44 (1929), 279-89, 444-53, 45 (1930), 92-101, 444-63.

Barlow, F., *The English Church, 1000-1166, A History of the Later Anglo-Saxon Church*, 2nd edn. (London and New York: Longman, 1979).

Barlow, F., *The English Church, 1066-1154, A History of the Anglo-Norman Church* (London and New York: Longman, 1979).

Barrow, J., art. 'Hereford', in A. Baudrillart et al., *Dictionnaire d'Histoire et de Géographie Ecclésiastiques* (Paris: Letouzey & Ané, 1909 ff.): 23 (1990), cols. 1407-17.

Barrow, J., 'A Lotharingian in Hereford: Bishop Robert's reorganisation of the church of Hereford, 1079-1095', in D. Whitehead (ed.), *Medieval Art, Architecture and Archaeology at Hereford, British Archaeological Association Conference Transactions* 15 (1995), 29-49.

Cannon, J., *Cathedral: The English Cathedrals and the World that Made Them, 600-1540* (London: Constable & Robinson, 2007).

Capes, W. W. (ed.), *Charters and Records of Hereford Cathedral [840-1421]* (Hereford: Cantilupe Society 3, 1908).

Edwards, K., *The English Secular Cathedrals in the Middle Ages* (Manchester: Manchester University Press, 1949; 2nd edn., New York: Barnes & Noble, 1967).

Havergal, F. T., *Fasti Herefordenses, and other Antiquarian Memorials of Hereford* ... with illustrations by G. C. Haddon (Edinburgh: R. Clark, 1869).

Hillaby, J., 'The origins of the diocese of Hereford', *Transactions of the Woolhope Naturalists' Field Club* 48 (1994), 23-36.

Hillaby, J., 'Leominster and Hereford: The origins of the diocese', in D. Whitehead (ed.), *Medieval Art, Architecture and Archaeology at Hereford, British Archaeological Association Conference Transactions* 15 (1995), 1-14.

Hills, G. M., 'The architectural history of Hereford Cathedral', *Journal of the British Archaeological Association* 27 (1871), 46-84.

Hoyt, R. S., art. 'Hereford, Ancient See of', in *New Catholic Encyclopedia*, 6 (New York: McGraw Hill, 1967), 1062.

Le Neve, J., *Fasti Ecclesiae Anglicanae, 1300-1541, 2 Hereford Diocese*, ed. Joyce M. Horn (London: Institute of Historical Research, 1962).

Le Neve, J., *Fasti Ecclesiae Anglicanae, 1066-1300, 8 Hereford Diocese*, ed. Julia S. Barrow (London: Institute of Historical Research, 2002).

Malpas, A., et al. (eds.), *The Early Church in Herefordshire, Proceedings of a Conference held at Leominster*, June 2000 (Leominster: Leominster History Study Group for Leominster Historical Society, 2001).

Marshall, G., *Hereford Cathedral, its Evolution and Growth* (Worcester: Littlebury & Co., 1951).

Mynors, R. A. B., and Thomson, R. M., *Catalogue of the Manuscripts of Hereford Cathedral Library, with Contributions on the Bindings by Michael Gullick* (published on behalf of the Dean and Chapter of Hereford Cathedral by D. S. Brewer (an imprint of Boydell & Brewer Ltd, Woodbridge, Suffolk), 1993).

Nichols, S., and Thurlby, M., 'Notes on the Romanesque Capitals from the East Arch of the Presbytery of Hereford Cathedral', *Friends of Hereford Cathedral, 51st Annual Report for the Year Ending 31 March 1985*, 14-26.

Rawlinson, R., *The History and Antiquities of the City and Cathedral-Church of Hereford ... with lists of the Principal Dignitaries; and an Appendix consisting of several ... original papers* (London, 1717).

Royal Commission on the Historical Monuments of England, *An Inventory of the*

Historical Monuments in Herefordshire, 3 vols. (London: HMSO, 1931-4): 1 (South-West), 90a- 117b.

Shoesmith, R., Hoverd, T., and Macklin, S., *Hereford Cathedral, Alterations to the Bishop's Cloister/Lady Arbour to house the Mappa Mundi and Chained Library Display: an Archaeological Report, including a Reinterpretation of the Losinga Chapel* (Hereford: City of Hereford Archaeological Unit, Hereford Archaeology Series 238, June 1996).

Thurlby, M., 'A note on the Romanesque Sculpture at Hereford Cathedral and the Herefordshire School of Sculpture', *Burlington Magazine* 126 (1984), 233-4.

Thurlby, M., *The Herefordshire School of Romanesque Sculpture*, 6th reprint (Woonton, Herefordshire: Logaston Press, 2013).

The following is a list of the titles published in this series by Hymns A & M; all (except double-size ones) are between 48 and 64 pages. Nos 1-58 were published by Grove Books Ltd, Ridley Hall Road, Cambridge CB3 9HU, and a complete list of those can be found on www.jointliturgicalstudies.hymnsam.co.uk, where you can also order past editions.

1   Roger Beckwith, *Daily and Weekly Worship – Jewish to Christian* (1987)
2   Paul Bradshaw (ed), *The Canons of Hippolytus* (1987)
3   Colin Buchanan (ed), *Modern Anglican Ordination Rites* (1987)
4   James Empereur, *Models of Liturgical Theology* (1987)
5   Thomas Talley (ed), *A Kingdom of Priests: Liturgical Formation of the People of God* (1988)
6   Colin Buchanan (ed), *The Bishop in Liturgy: An Anglican Symposium* (1988)
7   Phillip Tovey, *Inculturation: The Eucharist in Africa* (1988)
8   Paul Bradshaw (ed), *Essays in Early Eastern Initiation* (1988)
9   John Baldovin, *The Liturgy of the Church in Jerusalem* (1989)
10   Donald Withey (ed), *Adult Initiation* (1989)
11   John Fenwick, *'The Missing Oblation': The Contents of the Early Antiochene Anaphora* (1989)
12   Paul Rorem, *Calvin and Bullinger on the Lord's Supper* (1989)
13-14   (double-volume) W. Jardine Grisbrooke, *The Liturgical Portions of the Apostolic Constitutions: A Text for Students* (1990)
15   David Holeton (ed), *Liturgical Inculturation in the Anglican Communion* (1990)
16   Douglas Davies, *Cremation Today and Tomorrow* (1990)
17   Adrian Burdon, *The Preaching Service – the Glory of Methodism* (1991)
18   David Power, *Irenaeus of Lyon on Baptism and Eucharist* (1991)
19   Grant Sperry-White, *The Testamentum Domini: A Text for Students* (1991)
20   Gordon Jeanes, *The Origins of the Roman Rite* (1992)
21   Bosco Peters, *The Eucharist in New Zealand* (1992)
22-23   (double-volume) Ed Foley, *Music in the Early Church* (1992)
24   Paul James, *Eucharistic Presidency* (1993)
25   Ric Barrett-Lennard, *The Sacramentary of Sarapion of Thmuis: A Text for Students* (1993)
26   Phillip Tovey, *Communion Outside the Eucharist* (1993)
27   David Holeton (ed), *Revising the Eucharist: Groundwork for the Anglican Communion* (1994)
28   David Gitari (ed) *The Kanamai Statement 'African Culture and Anglican Liturgy' with Introduction, Papers read at Kanamai and a First Response* (1994)
29-30   (double-volume) Anita Stauffer, *On Baptismal Fonts: Ancient and Modern* (1994)
31   Fritz West, *The Comparative Liturgy of Anton Baumstark* (1995)
32   Alan Kreider, *Worship and Evangelism in Pre-Christendom* (1995)
33   Maxwell Johnson, *Liturgy in Early Christian Egypt* (1995)

66 Anthony Gelston, *The Psalms in Christian Worship: Patristic Precedent and Anglican Practice* (2008)

67 Mark Dalby, *Infant Communion from the Reformation to the Present Day* (2009)

68 Colin Buchanan (ed), *The Hampton Court Conference and the 1604 Book of Common Prayer* (2009)

69 Trevor Lloyd, James Steven and Phillip Tovey, *Social Science Methods in Contemporary Liturgical Research: An Introduction* (2010)

70 Alistair Stewart, *Two Early Egyptian Liturgical Papyri: The Deir Balyzeh Papyrus and the Barcelona Papyrus* (2010)

71 Kenneth Stevenson (ed), *Anglican Marriage Rites: A Symposium* (2011)

72 Andrew Atherstone, *Charles Simeon on the Excellence of the Liturgy* (2011)

73 Alan Griffiths, *Ordo Romanus Primus: Latin Text and Translation* (2012)

74 Trevor Lloyd (ed) *Rites Surrounding Death: The Palermo Statement with Commentary* (2012)

75 Mark Dalby, *Admission to Communion: The Approaches of the Late Medievals and the Reformers* (2013)

76 Dominic Keech, *Gaudius of Brescia on Baptism and the Eucharist* (2013)

77 Thomas O'Loughlin (ed), *Liturgical Language and Translation: The Issues Arising from the Revised Translation of the Roman Missal* (2014)

78 Paul Bradshaw and Juliette Day, *Further Essays on Early Eastern Initiation* (2014)

79 Phillip Tovey, *Eighteenth Century Anglican Confirmation: Renewing the Covenant of Grace* (2015)

80 Paul Bradshaw, *Ancient Church Orders* (2015)

81 Tim Stratford (ed), The Richard III Reinterment Liturgies (2016)

82 David Wallingford (ed. Gordon Jeanes), *The Decalogue in the Reformation Liturgies* (2016)

83 Neil O'Donoghue, *Liturgical Orientation: The Position of the President of the Eucharist* (2017)

84 James Steven, *Ambrose of Milan on Baptism: A Study of De Sacramentis and De Mysteriis* (2017)

85 Stephen R. Shaver, *Eucharistic Sacrifice as a Contested Category: A Cognitive Linguistics Approach* (2018)

Subscriptions

Annual subscription: £15 UK   £22 Worldwide

Joint Liturgical Studies is published twice a year, in May and October. Subscribe today to receive the next two issues direct to your home or office.

Call us: +44 (0)1603 785 910
Visit our website: jointliturgicalstudies.hymnsam.co.uk

Or complete this form and send it to:
Joint Liturgical Studies, Hymns Ancient & Modern, 13a Hellesdon Park Road, Norwich NR6 5DR

☐ I enclose a cheque for .... payable to Hymns Ancient & Modern Ltd.

Title................. First name..

Surname...

Address..

....

....

Postcode................................. Tel no...

Email..

How may we contact you?
We would like to keep you up-to-date with news and related offers from the Hymns Ancient & Modern Group. Please tick if you are happy for us to contact you: ☐ by mail   ☐ by email   ☐ by telephone